Globalisation and Africa in the Twenty-First Century

A Zambian Perspective

by

Singumbe Muyeba

authorHOUSE®

AuthorHouse™ UK Ltd.
500 Avebury Boulevard
Central Milton Keynes, MK9 2BE
www.authorhouse.co.uk
Phone: 08001974150

First published by AuthorHouse   2/19/2008

ISBN: 978-1-4343-6389-3 (sc)

Printed in the United States of America
Bloomington, Indiana

This book is printed on acid-free paper.

To my late mother for showing me the world
and for loving me and to Abigail, my God
sent best friend, life partner and love.

"The disparities between the world's richest and poorest nations are wider than ever… Nearly three billion people who are trying to survive on less than US \$2.00 a day deserve the chance for a better future.

Poverty is not just the greatest challenge to peace and stability in the 21st century but our greatest moral challenge as well…

Trying to turn back the clock and reverse the process of globalization will not solve the problems of the world as integration into the global economy still has a huge potential for improving human welfare…

Realizing this potential obliges us to work for a better globalization- one that is more inclusive, and seeks a better balancing of the risks and benefits. There is an urgent need to develop a political concept for one world, to guide and shape the process of globalization…

Globalization requires co-operation along with institutions to organize its many forms and to engage true commitment and support to the world's people, based on shared principles and rules… International decision making should be seen to respect national and local responsibilities, regions and cultures."

Horst Kobler

Former Managing Director of the International Monetary Fund[1]

PREFACE

My parents and elderly relatives used to tell me stories of how prosperous and enjoyable life was after independence and into the early 80s for our country. They often bragged about the many free things the government provided, especially the subsidised mealie-meal (staple maize meal) and schooling. It was the good life of the good old days. However, my experience growing up in Zambia during the 1990s exposed me to what I came to learn as the worst case scenario of poverty ever encountered in the history of that country. The 1990s were laden with extreme hardship for the people of Zambia and Sub Saharan Africa in general. Thousands of people lost their jobs as companies shut down one after the other. Many more public enterprises were privatized. The new private owners, seeking to significantly reduce costs and maximize profits, scaled down on their workforce by retrenching a number of the employees they found. The *World Development Report 2002*[2] reported that poverty in Zambia affected 86 per cent of the country's population.

On the ground, we saw a sudden wave of people becoming unemployed and a sudden increase in sicknesses and deaths. I remember that before the early 90s, a funeral was such a rare occurrence. When we saw one, we often stood by the roadside as the funeral procession passed in a show of respect for the dead. This practice gradually ended because suddenly there were too many funerals than one could afford to stop for and respect. Both my father and mother lost their jobs unexpectedly. As these events occurred, people viewed them as isolated occurrences. But I felt that there was more than meets the eye in the general picture. As my first Sociology lecturer would put it, I saw "the general in the particular and the strange in the familiar".

As time went by, we heard of new prominent concepts such as privatisation, budget cuts on public expenditure and removal of government subsidies.

Wallowing in the ambience, comfort and constant stability, we unbelievably saw the changes begin to take place. We heard of government retrenchments in an effort to scale down the bureaucracy and noticed a trend of price increases begin to unfold due to economic liberalisation. Loss of jobs was accompanied by increases in prices on essential commodities. People were thrown into destitution and the phenomenon of having one meal for the day was introduced in our homes. We were also informed of our countries' debt servicing obligations which implied that more of our money would go off public social expenditure. Internationally, the World Bank told us that we were living on less than US $1.00 a day and were in extreme poverty.

Many questions arose out of the 1990s, a time of rapid socio-economic decline. Zambians and Sub Saharan Africans in general are still trying to find answers after this tragic and shocking period, seven years into the third millennium. This is what this book is all about. It is a voice in search of answers for the many socio-economic questions that arose out of the experiences of the 1990s to the turn of the century and into the twenty first century.

In the book, I hope to identify the general ills of our society that became evident out of the socio-economic dislocation and to suggest ways such as cultural change and international cooperation through which Africa can achieve socio-economic development by working with the institutions whose policies birthed such misery for us in the 90s.

At the turn of the century, of highest concern to world leaders during the United Nations Millennium Summit was the reduction of hunger and extreme poverty in its many dimensions by 2015. The solution was the adoption of eight Millennium Development Goals (MDGs). I believe the Eighth MDG is a major panacea for Africa in the twenty-first century.

My inspiration for writing this book essentially came from my formative years. My mother took me along on her business trips abroad. The travelling experiences opened my mind to two worlds; that of the rich and that of the poor. The last stroke that broke the camels back was a trip to New York in 2001, during my undergraduate studies at the University of Zambia. It raised two questions. Firstly, why is their so much poverty suffered by people in Africa when people in London and New York etc are prospering? Secondly, what are the solutions to the problem of poverty in Zambia and Sub Saharan Africa? To answer these questions, I committed myself to years of learning, mostly through broad study- I am still learning- and experience working and living in the poorest province of Zambia. Therefore, what I share in this book is what I have learned so far.

This book is written for that African who asked the questions I asked, who survived the 1990s and who lived to tell his/her own story. Leaders, intellectuals, government employees and personnel from international development agencies, students and all those concerned about the development of the African continent must acquaint themselves with the contents of these passages of writing. The reality of the sufferings and the urgency with which the problem of extreme poverty has to be addressed cannot be over-emphasized. I accept responsibility for any errors of fact and misinterpretation that may be imbedded in this piece of work.

ACKNOWLEDGEMENTS

I thank God for giving me this knowledge and opportunity to share it in this manner. My heartfelt gratitude goes to my wife, Abigail Kabandula Muyeba. I wish to express my deepest thanks with my deepest love for the tremendous support and encouragement I could never get from any other person. I would also like to thank my uncle, Professor and Ambassador Mwelwa C. Musambachime, Aunty Phoebe and family for being an inspiration to me and for all the support and care. I acknowledge all my colleagues in the United Nations for their contribution to my scope of knowledge during my internship and consequent work as a United Nations Volunteer. Due gratitude also goes to my lecturers at University of Zambia, Professor J.C. Momba, Dr W. N. Mafuleka, Mr. M. Lipalile and many others for all the work they have done in shaping my philosophy. Thanks to Professor F.W.B Akuffo and Mr Donald Chanda for criticisms and proofreading. Thanks for the support from my father, Mr. Richard Muyeba. I appreciate my sisters Mulela, Mwansa and brother Moses for their endurance. I thank God for using you; bless you. I cannot go without thanking Mr. and Mrs. Kana and Mr and Mrs Kabaso of Kasama. I thank my friends Brian Mwanza, George Mwale, Lucy Mulesa, Chilambe Katuta, Malama Chalwe and Timothy Phiri. To all those I could not mention, I appreciate your contributions to my personal development and God bless you.

Singumbe Muyeba

CONTENTS

PREFACE ix
ACKNOWLEDGEMENTS xiii
ACRONYMS xvii
Introduction 1
   Trends in the Twentieth Century 1
   The State of the World at the End
   of the Twentieth Century 3
   Hope amidst Challenges for Africa
   in the Twenty First Century 6
**Ills of African Culture and Society in the Twenty
First Century: A Zambian Perspective** 9
   Presidentialism. 10
   Low Productivity and Lack of Culture
   of Surplus Productivity. 16
   Ethnicism and Clientelism 21
Globalisation 31
   Defining Globalization 31
   The Washington Consensus 33
   Main Players in Globalisation. 35
   Mechanisms of Globalisation 36
   Internationalization of Production 36
   Privatization. 39
   International Trade 41
   Global Finance 43
   Rapid Development in Information
   and Communication Technology 43
   Political Globalization. 45
   Globalisation and Production. 46

Multinational Corporations (MNCs) in Africa in the Twenty First Century 49

    Cutting down Production Costs. 52

International Financial Institutions and Africa in the Twenty First Century 57

    The Bretton Woods Institutions. 57

    Africa and The Structural Adjustment Programs . . . 59

Africa, Production and International Trade in the Twenty First Century 69

    International Trade and Africa in the 21st Century . . . 72

    Sub Saharan Africa's Challenges
    in International Trade 74

    Consequences of Low Productivity
    and Low participation in International Trade 78

Case Study of Zambia 81

    Low productivity in Zambia. 81

    Origins of Culture of Low Productivity 83

    Production Structure of Zambia 84

    Individual Productivity 86

    Social Consequences of Lack of Productivity
    in Zambia. 87

Cultural Change 93

    Presidentialism. 94

    Ethnicism and Clientelism 96

    Low Productivity and Lack of Culture
    of Surplus Productivity. 97

Economic Cooperation with the IMF, World Bank and WTO 105

International Cooperation: the Panacea in the 8th Millennium Development Goal and in Africa's Survival in the Twenty First Century . . . 115

Conclusion 129

Endnotes 137

ACRONYMS

AAC	Anglo American Corporation
ADB	African Development Bank
AGOA	African Growth and Opportunity Act
AIDS	Acquired Immunodeficiency Syndrome
ARV	Anti Retroviral
BOZ	Bank of Zambia
COMESA	Common Market for East and Southern Africa
CSO	Central Statistics Office
CSPR	Civil Society for Poverty Reduction
DfID	Department for International Development
DHS	Demographic Health Survey
EIA	Environmental Impact Assessment
EU	European Union
FAO	Food and Agriculture Organisation
FBO	Faith Based Organisations
FDI	Foreign Direct Investment
FHH	Female Headed Household
FTA	Free Trade Area
GDP	Gross Domestic Product
GRZ	Government of the Republic of Zambia
HFS	Health Facility Survey
HIPC	Highly Indebted Poor Country
HIV	Human Immunodeficiency Virus
HPI	Human Poverty Index
HRC	Permanent Human Rights Commission
ICT	Information and Communication Technology
IEC	Information, Education and Communication
IMF	International Monetary Fund
IMR	Infant Mortality Rate

ISI	Import Substitution Industrialisation
JICA	Japan International Cooperation Agency
KCM	Konkola Copper Mines
LCMS	Living Conditions Monitoring Survey
LuSE	Lusaka Stock Exchange
MDGs	Millennium Development Goals
MFNP	Ministry of Finance and National Planning
MMR	Maternal Mortality Rate
MTCT	Mother to Child Transmission
NGO	Non-Governmental Organisation
OECD	Organisation for Economic Cooperation and Development
PRGF	Poverty Reduction and Growth Facility
PRP	Poverty Reduction Programme
PRSP	Poverty Reduction Strategy Paper
PSRP	Public Service Reform Programme
SADC	Southern African Development Community
SAP	Structural Adjustment Programme
STD	Sexually Transmitted Disease
STI	Sexually Transmitted Infection
TB	Tuberculosis
UN	United Nations
UNDP	United Nations Development Programme
UNHCR	United Nations High Commissioner for Refugees
UNICEF	United Nations Children's Fund

Chapter One

Introduction

Trends in the Twentieth Century

On February 24, 1995, a thirteen year old boy lost his mother to Meningitis and prolonged depression. The mother worked for Zambia Airways, the national airline. A few months earlier, on a seemingly uneventful day, she as usual, got to Ndeke House. To her dismay, policemen had surrounded her office headquarters. They did not allow her and her colleagues to go into their offices. Zambia Airways Corporation was liquidated and over 3,000 people worldwide suddenly lost their jobs. I was that teenager and my father also lost his job on that same day in 1994.

The 1990s were not good years for me and my country Zambia. I learned from a copy of the Post Newspaper in 1996 that my mother was listed as one among thousands of people who had died of depression caused by the loss of their jobs in the defunct companies. This occurrence was only but a tip of the iceberg of the devastating social consequences of the policies imposed by the Washington based International Monetary Fund and the World Bank on the country. As a result of privatisation, reduction in public expenditure, including removal of subsidies on health services, essential foods and commodities, Zambians had suddenly begun to die in large numbers. Yet they had no idea that their deaths had anything to do with white collar policy makers sitting behind their desks in Washington DC, shaping the phenomenon we have come to call globalisation.

As I grew up in much hardship and difficulty, I learned that these devastating effects did not only affect my country but Sub-Saharan Africa as well. Later, I learned of effects such as riots carried out in Zambia in 1986, across Africa in the 90s, to the Far East as well as South America in protest against the two institutions' policies.

Today I look back and say I have survived Structural Adjustment Programmes and by the grace of God, learned and lived to tell the story the way I understand it.

The experiences above forced me to ask vital questions to shape my philosophy of life. I asked questions such as; What is going on? Why are we suffering as a people and a country? Who is responsible for our circumstances? What are the solutions? And what can we do about it?

I devoted myself to answering these questions as my journey through life. I hope I share it well that together in Zambia and Sub Saharan Africa, we may understand better our country's circumstances and work together to help Africa survive globalisation. Here is the story that I tell knowing that many others who could have told it better did not live to have the chance to.

The State of the World at the End of the Twentieth Century

From 1989, the world witnessed dramatic events that would usher in the twenty first century. After the fall of the Berlin Wall in November 1991, the world was never to be the same again. The once great Soviet empire, disintegrated. In the words of Winston Churchill, the "Iron Curtain" had been drawn. History recorded the triumph of capitalism, liberalism, democracy and the rebirth of the commitment to and advocacy for fundamental human rights and freedoms.

As opposed to a bi-polar international power structure that obtained during the cold war, the world witnessed the emergence of the United States of America as the sole superpower, a champion of democracy, freedoms and human rights. No nation could match the political, economic and military power of this proud nation.

This unfolding scenario had its own implications for Africa. There was a sudden wave of democratisation and economic liberalisation across Africa. The changes were mostly unexpected and came as a surprise to the African people. Employees in public enterprises and institutions of governance suddenly found themselves unemployed in a wave of retrenchment programmes under public service reforms. This was coupled with the removal of subsidies on essential commodities that included staple foods. Nothing was for free anymore. More accurately put, everything had to be paid for. It was a major social transformation for most.

Following closely behind was another wave of Structural Adjustment Programmes (SAP) sweeping through the continent. The multilateral donors through the International Monetary Fund (IMF) and the World Bank had identified that poor countries were in stagnation and in some circumstances in retrogression due to structural rigidities in their planned economies and governance systems. Therefore, the poor countries had to adjust their economies by removing the structural rigidities through trade liberalization, privatization of state enterprises, implementation of policies of good governance, public service reforms (PSR) and overhaul of fiscal policies.

At the close of the Twentieth Century, the global economy prospered in a scenario comparable to the boom years just before the great depression of the 1930s.

Globalisation rapidly intensified the interdependence of economies leading to an economic boom. Two views emerged; on the one hand, scholars argued that globalization was a new phenomenon propelling the global economy; on the other, scholars argued that globalization was an old process that merely emerged in a more intensified and complex process during the late twentieth century. There was an increase in international trade, internationalization of production processes, global travel, cultural exchanges and rapid development of Information and Communications Technology (ICT) as one of the fastest mode of communication especially through the internet. During the boom years, international trade between the United States, The European Union (EU), Japan, plus the Asian Tigers grew rapidly. Africa accounted for a mere 2 per cent of that trade.

Most of Africa had little or no involvement in these developments. Approximately 98 per cent of global trade took place without the involvement of any African country[3]. Of the 2 per cent in which Africa participated, over 1 per cent was South Africa's and Nigeria's share of world trade. The rest of the 1 per cent was divided among the 53 African countries.

Then, like the rule of thumb of 'boom' before 'bust', at the turn of the century, starting from Japan in 1998 to be specific, the "bubble burst" – again - like in the 1930s. The inflated market prices of shares in the United States soon revealed their real value. In panic, investors in Japan withdrew their investments at a record rate and the global economy went into recession.

At the turn of the century, terrorism against the United States and Europe increased forcing diverted focus of the international community from Africa's development to the war on terrorism. Africa suffered, having no strong capital base of its own to determine its own destiny. Its survival in the global economy was beginning to be threatened.

At about the same time, the oil industry degenerated with oil prices souring to historically record highs. It was a time comparable to the 1973 oil price increases that shocked and set many African countries off their development courses for decades and into the twenty first century, threatening Africa's survival. Will history repeat itself? Will it be that for the next three decades, the development path of the African countries will be jeopardized with these compounding factors?

Hope amidst Challenges for Africa
in the Twenty First Century

As opposed to the situation obtaining at the twilight of the twentieth century, at the dawn of the twenty first century was a renewed commitment to Africa's development. This was demonstrated in the adoption of the Millennium Development Goals, the establishment of the Blair Commission on Africa by former British Prime Minister Tony Blair, with the help of rock star Bob Geldof and Chancellor of the Ex-chequer Gordon Brown. The G8 group of Countries in the 2002 Monterrey Consensus further renewed their pledge to increase their GDP allocation to Official Development Assistance to 0.7 per cent of their income.

There was also renewed commitment by African leaders with the establishment of NEPAD, a home grown African development initiative. Further, the dawn of the Twenty First Century witnessed the transformation of the Organisation of African Unity (OAU) into the new and invigorated African Union (AU). The AU promised a renewed commitment to good governance and human rights for Africa's development.

However, levels of international cooperation for international peace and sustainable development between Africa and the West remained within the confines of African leaders' "facile satisfactions of international diplomacy" as described by Israeli statesman and diplomat Abba Eban[4]. African leaders continued to pay less and less attention to practical international cooperation with the west as an essential tool of addressing Africa's problems of illiteracy, starvation, rampant disease, and want.

[5] "Third world leaders would be on more solid ground in their discourse with the west if they would take their stand on mutual cooperation between the developed and developing worlds rather than on pretensions of moral superiority. The developing countries do not always offer other nations social visions worthy of emulation."

Africa in the twenty first century faces crises that are threatening to the very existence of its people. Perhaps the most important is the HIV/AIDS pandemic dubbed as the greatest leadership challenge of Africa by the United Nations[6]. The disease is threatening to annihilate people in the Sub-Saharan African region. It must be borne in mind that during the first years of the epidemic (towards the end of the 1970s and at the beginning of the 1980s) the scourge had its epicentre in the Sub Saharan African region, specifically in the present day DR Congo and Uganda. Though scientific progress has been made in terms of the level of awareness on the disease and anti-retroviral therapy, finding a cure and a vaccine remain distant even with the scientific advancement of the twenty first century. The tests for a vaccine are still in their infancy while infection and prevalence rates continue to rise rapidly in this region. I have avoided writing much on this subject as current literature on HIV/AIDS in the Sub Saharan African region in relation to development is overwhelming. However, this is not to undermine the gravity of the effects of HIV/AIDS on Africa's participation in globalisation and its survival in the twenty first century.

While the global picture offered answers to the questions I had, I decided to look within ourselves as an individual, a people and a continent while carrying the answers the global picture had to offer.

The fulcrum of this book is that Africa is responsible for its circumstances and needs to address the cultural and socio-economic ills within its societies first and then the challenges of global integration internationally to survive in globalisation. The underlying solutions are that a deliberate African cultural transformation and globalization offer an opportunity for Africans to survive the twenty first century and beyond. Mutual international cooperation between Sub Saharan Africa and the west is the underlying framework for these solutions to Sub Saharan Africa's and Zambia's challenge of achieving sustainable development.

Chapter Two

Ills of African Culture and Society in the Twenty First Century: A Zambian Perspective

During the 1990s, I was amused by what kind of posters I used to see. Most of them had a moral teaching about them using a frightening message. Some would have a big word reading "STOP VANDALISM" and others would read "CORRUPTION DOES NOT PAY" or "CRIME DOES NOT PAY". Some would have a big military boot stepping on hands about to pass a bribe, it was magnificent. Of course these posters are still here today albeit in different forms. We see more of HIV/AIDS posters though. I believe the posters were well intentioned; to create awareness on a societal vice. But I also believe that the posters addressed the wrong problems in our society. The effect of instilling fear in people is that they get threatened only for a while, then they get used to the threats and then get back to these vices. I believe the vices are worse today than in the 90s because as an example, Transparency International (TI) ranked Zambia the eleventh most corrupt country in the world at the end of 2005[7]. To address a vice in society, one must go to the crux. The following ills of African culture and society have been identified by scholars and leaders whom I agree with.

Presidentialism

The structure of government as a mechanism of political representation determines how the executive is constituted, how the legislature is composed and the scope of separation of powers. According to the Africa Governance Report, "In Africa there are three types of governmental structure: presidential, parliamentary and hybrid. The hybrid system is the most common[8].

The presidential system has a single executive, the president, who is usually directly elected by the people and who, as the fulcrum of power, solely appoints a cabinet. The president has control of parliament. However, the principle of separation of powers is usually clearly pronounced in a presidential system. Benin, Togo, Burkina Faso, Cameroon, Gabon, The Gambia, Malawi, Mozambique, Nigeria, Uganda and Zimbabwe have the presidential system.

The hallmark of the parliamentary system is a fusion of legislative and executive powers. The president has mostly ceremonial functions as head of state.

However, many African countries have a hybrid governmental structure that combines the two ends of the spectrum from elements of the parliamentary to those of the presidential systems. These countries include Botswana, Chad, Egypt, Ghana, Kenya, Mali, Namibia, Niger, Senegal, South Africa, Tanzania and Zambia.

I have identified a fundamental ill of African societies in the form of a government system leaning on Presidentialism in the hybrid system, which is mixed with African traditional systems. In this system, the president possesses more of the elements of presidentialism and an African Chief, that is, powers to the extreme. It is also known as "Personalistic Rule". It is the manner in which power is traditionally exercised in Sub Saharan Africa. The politics in this system revolve around one big man instead of the modern rational bureaucratic form. In this system, nearly all executive and legislative power is concentrated in one ruler- the president. It further connotes the omnipotence of the president. The power of the president in Africa possesses a sacred and all-encompassing character.

In Personalistic Rule, there exists a lack of distinction between the public and private domains of the institution of the presidency. This means that the modern bureaucratic institutions are invaded and assimilated by the private domain of the ruler, hence the employment of the term. In the cases of Togo and The Democratic Republic Congo, the evidence of this system went to a conspicuous extent, in which the Togolese ruler, Gnasimbe Eyadema groomed and handed down the presidency to his son, Faure Gnasimbe as did DR Congo's Laurent Desire Kabila groom and hand down the office to Joseph Kabila. This situation is in the making in Senegal where Abdoulaye Wade has been grooming his son.

"The origins of this all-encompassing concept of power are located in a social framework that is based on networks of patronage; informal personal connections of kin found in African culture through which African leaders distribute resources"[9].

Theoretically as well as practically, presidentialism emanates from the fusion of African traditional practice and modern organisation management practice. Max Weber rightly described the undocumented system of traditional authority and the legal rational authority run under a constitution. However, he did not foresee the potential of fusion between these systems. Neither did he foresee their potential to bring about the personalistic rule of presidentialism that has infected Sub Saharan Africa.

Today, the presidentialism of personalistic rule exhibits a common deep seated African practice in which the ruler is the custodian of all public resources of the land. Such a concept has formed a complex mix with modern forms of government as introduced by colonial rule in the nineteenth and twentieth centuries. This concept of power has gradually been naturalised and internalised into Sub Saharan African culture and people. It is now a typical form of modern Sub Saharan African government.

Virtually all presidentialist regimes have experienced authoritarianism as well as military coups. Colonialism in Zambia and the consequent regime of the country's first president, Dr. Kenneth David Kaunda, were not lacking in the definition of authoritarianism. This is not to dispel the country's successes during he's presidency. However, Dr. Kaunda's rule was charismatically spiced with such undemocratic slogans as "One Zambia, One Nation;

One Nation, One leader; and that Leader, Kenneth Kaunda *uwa muyayaya* (life long president).

Since authoritarian regimes, juntas included, are in essence presidentialist regimes, one can soundly conclude that Presidentialism as it is today in Zambia was not caused by the authoritarian regime of the 70 year colonial rule, nor the 27 years under Dr. Kaunda. Neither was it caused by the failed military coups. However, there is no doubt that these periods played an essential part in concretising the institutions of a presidentialist regime. This essentially refers to the concentration of power in the executive and the dispelling of the principle of separation of powers.

Personalistic rule or Presidentialism's origins in Zambia are therefore attributed to the interaction of socio-cultural forces that emanated from traditional forms of rule and colonial rule. In the traditions of the 72 tribes found in Zambia, it is the rule and the norm that the paramount chief or the chief decides who acquires land and where. It is his prerogative to distribute land and the proceeds. His word suffices for all his subjects to obey and for the society to carry out his decree. In short, he is that one big man at the centre of society. So is it for the nation at large. The presidency in Zambia carries similar characteristics. The Zambian president's power ranges from the appointment of Cabinet Ministers without prior parliamentary approval, Permanent Secretaries (who ideally should be technocrats appointed on merit and not by patronage) to diplomatic personnel also without prior approval or consent of the National Assembly.

Demonstrably, Presidentialism in Africa has not been successful in bringing about political development and socio-economic progress because of its Personalistic tendencies. In fact, it has done the exact opposite. This is where there is a clash of cultures.

A key phenomenon to understand is that what the Sub Saharan African people view as a natural part of culture (Personalistic rule, clientelism and ethnicism described below) is what is viewed as corruption by Western definition.

On the one hand, Western and international public institutions ideally observe a clear distinction between the public and private domains of the office bearer of the presidency and generally public office. In fact there are well developed laws and legal institutions that prosecute against those that utilize public funds and equipment for personal gain in western countries.

In Sub Saharan Africa on the other hand, such a distinction is blur. These institutions are not fully developed and where they are, they are under-funded. Often, their operations are interfered with by the politicians that appoint them. For example, to investigate the alleged corrupt practices of his predecessor's administration, the president of Zambia created a Task Force on Corruption. In itself, such an act constituted a realization of the absence of an independent specialized agency, and the under-funding and over-burdened reality of the police force and the Anti-Corruption Commission- which are far from independent.

The blur distinction between the public and private domains in African public institutions is further exacerbated by the existence of an inadequate legal framework and legal institutions. A simple example is that instructions or commands from the Head of State to any official are in many circumstances made by a simple word of mouth requiring no documentation. The problem is compounded by the fact that this system is present at every level of public office as I will show in my discourse on clientelism.

Whereas it is important for Africa to safeguard its tradition and culture, so is it imperative to realise the impact of personalistic rule and/or presidentialism on Zambia and Sub Saharan Africa in the age of globalisation. Personalistic rule has had enormous consequences on African government and it will work to the detriment of the African people and culture in the 21st century. The sooner African governments realise this, the better the chances of survival in globalisation.

What is the basic reason why presidentialism has been successful in the United States of America and unsuccessful in Sub Saharan Africa? Fred Riggs[10] suggests a hypothesis that might explain why. He argues that "the newer presidentialist regimes [Sub Saharan Africa included] may have rejected, as -undemocratic- some practices that, perhaps unintentionally, have helped American presidentialism to survive. If so, these regimes were unconsciously caught in a double bind: to be more -democratic- involved taking risks that could lead to dictatorship, whereas to perpetuate representative government meant accepting some patently undemocratic rules". In other words, what Riggs is pointing out is that the separation of powers has successfully worked alongside the American system of presidentialism. Yet it was viewed as one that could lead to dictatorship of the legislature over the executive arm in Africa.

Riggs goes on to argue that "The American constitutional system based on the separation of powers was modelled on a transitional stage in the evolution of democracy as experienced in 18th century England. With Kings struggling to retain power against insurgent parliamentary forces, a precarious imbalance of power existed which the Founding Fathers copied in America, but sought to stabilize by an ingenious though precarious system of checks and balances". In comparison, the Sub Saharan African system went from colonialism, by all means and ends authoritarian, through independence struggle to presidential system. The concept of separation of powers, though introduced in part was never fully appreciated and was not given an opportunity to develop. In addition, colonial parliaments effectively excluded the native population, who were clearly in the majority, from effective representation.

Low Productivity and Lack of Culture of Surplus Productivity

I have observed an ill of our African culture that has had devastating consequences upon our economic and social progress. It will undoubtedly have catastrophic consequences for Africa in its quest to survive globalization. It is the African attitude toward production. Generally, we have a culture of producing enough only for consumption. Individuals, young and old alike, embrace a perspective that governs their thinking under which they address their current needs. Tomorrow, it will be the same routine. It is a mental construct and a psychological trait. It is a semi-unproductive character trait.

In the likeness of John Stuart Mill's writing in his *Principles of Political Economy[11]*, I use the phrase semi-unproductive not in the light of disparagement... The labour of officers of government, of the army and navy, of physicians, lawyers, teachers, musicians, dancers, actors, domestic servants, ... ought not to be "stigmatized" as unproductive, an expression which you may regard as synonymous with wasteful or worthless.

In other words, I use the phrase semi- unproductive here as a descriptive term of the underlying character trait of lack of concern for surplus high quality production-otherwise known as subsistence culture. It is a form of production concerned with meeting immediate needs without regard to storing for future purposes or for sale for purposes of making a profit; which I have identified as the character of many of our African people. Allow me to add that the immediate needs met are entirely to do with drunkenness. I have held meetings with several community groups in Zambia. It is the common case that a quarter to half of the people present are drunk. The point is that most of what is raised from the little production goes to alcohol and substance abuse.

Following independence, several governments of the new African states adopted forms of the socialist system, generating a range of nomenclature, from Kaunda's Humanism to Nyerere's Ujaama to Senghor's Negritude.

These were semi-communist systems in which basic necessities were provided for free to the people during the post independence euphoria. There was free staple food in form of mealie meal in the case of Zambia, free education including pens, pencils and books, free biscuits, free train and bus rides for young people and so forth. Everyone who had done basic schooling was guaranteed employment in the government and other public enterprises. This is in addition to free accommodation for employees, free electricity, free water and free health services for all. And they could not be laid off work.

Over a long period of time, in some cases three or more decades, these free provisions became entrenched on the minds and way of life of Africans. Value and respect for work and a whole different work ethic ensued. There was a loss of a clear connection between work and earning a living as people were able to access basic necessities without working for them. As far as our people were concerned, it was the government's responsibility to take care of each of our needs without our paying for them.

This mental/cultural state is predominantly found in one of the most important economic sectors; agriculture. The majority of farmers produce only enough for consumption. According to the Selected Socio-Economic Indicators of the Central Statistics Office, sixty seven percent of Zambians for example live in rural areas. Their livelihood is in agriculture. At the same time, another fact is that the majority of people living in rural areas are non-commercial or subsistence farmers. The interaction of these factors demonstrates that the majority of people in rural areas produce their produce for consumption.

Little or no maize for example is stored to be used in the next year or two. This is the simple reason why Africa, and Zambia in particular has no food security.

This mental/cultural state is not only in agriculture. In the various offices, especially the public sector institutions, Africans do not put in their best. There is seldom satisfactory performance, and real struggle for public servants to provide public services. In most instances, our targets are not formally set and where they are, the culture is not to give more than what has been targeted. The standard or quality of work is below par. For example, in 2006, Transparency International Zambia Chapter ran publications in the print media on the process of obtaining a passport. According to the procedure, it is possible for one to obtain a passport in three days. But because of falling short of producing only enough, putting in the required effort, putting in only as much as has been asked for (perhaps less), a passport takes over two months to be processed. In addition, more importance is given to the avoidance of exposure of the broken rules and procedures than to the primary objective.

From another perspective, the majority of Africans do not consider the future as a factor in living their lives today. John S. Mbiti[12], a professor of Theology and Comparative Religion at Makerere University in Uganda wrote the following about African progress:

> ``Each African people has its own history. This history goes backwards, from a moment of intense experience back to a period beyond which nothing happens. In traditional African thought, there is no concept of history moving

forward, towards a future climax or towards the end of the world. Since the future is concerned only in terms of a couple of months, the future can open neither a golden age nor a state of radically different affairs. The notion of a messianic hope or the final destruction has no place in the traditional concept of history. Therefore, Africans do not believe in `progress,' in the idea that the development and activities and human achievements move from a lower to a higher degree."

Globalisation thrives on a country's ability to produce enough for its citizens to consume and leave a surplus for the external market, for that extra income which helps the Balance of Payments. Globalisation is based on the idea of a country interacting with another through the products and services (surplus) it offers. If African countries and our people produce enough only for subsistence, and we do not produce in surplus, how will we gain profits for use to obtain other goods and services not provided in our countries? Currently, Sub-Sahara African countries are almost net importers of goods and services of a wide variety. Investment in large and most industries are foreign. The funds being used by governments to import are basically aid funds. What will happen when donor fatigue worsens. There is need to improve our culture of production and even a bigger and much more urgent need to develop a culture of surplus production. Professor Mbiti continues:

> Through interaction with advanced wealth creating nations, Africans may learn about the nature of wealth and how to create it. The absence of a wealth-creation culture is the major obstacle to African societies realising their dream of industrialisation. They lack wealth-creating classes, either in the form of a bourgeoisie or a socialist bureaucracy. Given the propensity for corruption in societies where the

elites are impatient for personal wealth and modernity, the prospect of genuine socialism developing in Africa is small. Therefore, there is no viable alternative to the emergence of local bourgeoisie that can be a driving force for material development.

African nations need to face up to the harsh realities of surviving in a highly competitive global system. Some critics of globalisation and market economies present economic development and prosperity as human rights, things that come about simply because people are poor. The impression is created that the responsibility for transcending the poverty of underdeveloped nations lies with rich nations - all the poor need do is demand prosperity and sit back waiting to receive what they are due. This latter-day liberalism has not been helpful.

Many liberal opponents of globalisation harbour disdain for large-scale productive activities and dismiss notions like efficiency, productivity and growth as dogmas of greedy capitalists. But it is difficult to see how poor nation's economies can grow rapidly without striving to become more efficient producers. Similarly, it is hard to fathom how these nations can eradicate poverty without accelerated economic growth. By striving to keep pace with the tempo of globalisation African nations are more likely to develop the productive culture they need to attain their people's dream of modern material prosperity.

The prerequisite to trade in the international economy is surplus production. But in the age of globalization, where global capitalism reigns, each African, each Zambian is called to produce in whatever capacity. However, it is not just production but high quality surplus production.

Ethnicism and Clientelism

Most African states are multi-ethnic and multilingual, comprising ethnic groups of different sizes, culture and historical background. This came about as a result of migrations and the partition of Africa during the 1890s by European powers in their struggle for territorial dominance. In the process of these important events in African history, European colonialists drew borders, dividing Africa's land into territories on economic considerations rather than ethnicity. This led to the grouping of two or more different ethnic groups in a single territory. Some, as in the case of the Hutu, were divided in such a way that part of the group belonged to Rwanda while the other belonged to the neighbouring territory, Burundi. In other cases, two or more hostile groups were brought together into one territory as in the case of the Democratic Republic of Congo and Sudan. For a few countries such as Zambia, political hostilities based on ethnic identity are a recipe for peace in the sense that much ethnic diversity has brought a sustainable level of tolerance.

However, for the most part of Sub Saharan Africa, states have never known peace since obtaining independence because of ethnic rivalry. Having not known peace, they have never been set on a path to socio-economic development. One can also pinion that in all countries, ethnic differences have worked more to the detriment of development and efforts toward nation building. I believe that ethnicism is one among many factors that will work to the detriment of Africa's survival in the era of globalisation in the 21st Century simply because ethnicism works against peace and peace is a prerequisite to socio-economic development. Ethnic favouritism also violates laid down procedures based on merit hence is a recipe for more corruption- a major problem in African government.

In the words of Sociologist, Vilfredo Pareto[13], "the term ethnicity is one of the vaguest terms known to sociology." Talcott Parsons[14] puts it another way saying "it seems to be generally agreed that what we call ethnicity...is an extraordinarily elusive concept and very difficult to define in any precise way". However, many scholars have attempted to define it using different perspectives. For the purpose of this book, I have decided to use that provided by Osaghae[15] whose view is that ethnicity refers to the state of any "distinct group which possess amongst others, language, culture, myth of origin and territory which differentiates it from other groups".

One of the most prominent features of ethnicism is ethnocentrism. It refers to an individual's view of ones ethnicity as being superior and that all others that do not possess the same culture, historical background and linguistic attributes are inferior. This is true not only for Sub Saharan Africa, but is a factor unfortunately found in every ethnic grouping and culture worldwide. Therefore in government, individuals who subscribe to this view tend to make decisions that are favourable to people of the same ethnic identity as they are, at the expense of equitable distribution of public goods and services.

The ethnic identity and its limits affect the loyalty and personal choices of the individual who is fixed along the lines of ethnicity and clans. Ethnicism identifies the individual as anti-human, narrow and closed-minded. The ethnic person, instead of being judged on the basis of his contribution to universal human knowledge, is defined first and foremost only as a member of an ethnic group; as a Zulu, Tutsi, Hutu, Bemba, a Lozi or a Kaonde, etc. He is made to believe that his ethnic origin, geographical location, language and religion are particulars opposed to the interests of all other groups. He is to die as he was born, carrying his hate and prejudices. It is this identity, fiercely defended, that allowed colonial forces to set up one ethnic group against another, creating totally artificial ethnic warfare. Then, hatred and rivalry for "limited resources" began and has been extended to postcolonial times[16].

Today, the most prominent cause of political instability and chaos in Africa is ethnic conflict. Many more Africans have died as a result of inter-ethnic conflicts since independence than did at any equivalent time span during colonialism[17].

Ethnicity further boils down to ethnicisation. In his comprehensively inquisitive treaties entitled *What Went Wrong with Africa,* Roel Van Der Veen[18] described ethnicity as an obstacle to the development of democracy in Africa. Though Van Der Veen restricted his perspective to ethnicisation as an obstacle to democracy, ethnicism is also an obstacle to the wider objective of sustainable development. This is so in that the equitable distribution of goods and services is derailed by the ethnic group in power which concentrates the benefits of public goods and services to itself and to the exclusion of others. Take for example in Nigeria, ethnic rivalries between the Hausa, Ybo and Yoruba have time and again caused problems in the oil rich country where the Hausa feel left out on the proceeds. In Africa, ethnicism has tremendous repercussions on the current and future development efforts. Several well funded development projects have had funds disappear within the bureaucracy under the aid of complex ethnic connections. Broadly speaking, the reason is that Ethnicity permeates the entire spectrum of African culture and lifestyle in the twenty first century.

Political parties in Africa today are almost always aligned or identified with a particular ethnic group. In Zambia, John Mwanakatwe[19] wrote that President Kaunda's "biggest problem in post-independence times was to contain growing sectionalism [ethnicism] among members of his own political party at all levels." in fact, "in 1966, a number of UNIP members left to join the United Party which was largely lozi speaking in its leadership and support. Kaunda's boyhood friend, Simon Mwansa Kapwepwe resigned to form his own United Progressive Party, which was largely Bemba speaking. Ethnicism had reached depressing levels for the president to handle that he resigned as president of Zambia at the party's general conference at Mulungushi in 1967. Mwanakatwe states that "Kaunda was dismayed at the escalating sectional groupings within the party. Being by nature a highly emotional person, he had single-handedly taken a drastic decision to resign as President of Zambia as well as giving up the party post of president. He gave the following speech:

> Fellow countrymen, I have for the past several hours listened to the views expressed in this hall. I must say how deeply shocked I have been to realise for the first time how deeply divided the party is- and even more deeply shocked to learn that the division is purely along tribal lines.

> During my tenure of Office of President I have done all I could to try and point out that if we fall prey to tribalism, we might as well write off the Republic of Zambia. All my efforts have been in vain, all my efforts have been in vain. This afternoon I sent a note to the Attorney-General, James Skinner, asking him what legal steps are necessary before a Head of State can resign.[20]

As history records, the country almost went into a civil war based on ethnic lines but in the end, the president continued in his position for over twenty years. But that was not the end of ethnicism. In today's Zambia and Africa, it is not institutionalised officially as much as it is in practice. It is common knowledge that the United Party for National Development (UPND) is identified with the Tonga ethnic group such that when their first leader, Anderson Mazoka died, there were widespread calls for him to be replaced by a tribe mate. Indeed a relatively politically naïve Tonga businessman, Hikainde Hichilema was voted in as successor over the more experienced former deputy president of the party, Sakwiba Sikota. Sikota belonged to a different ethnic group. Further, the Patriotic Front (PF) is identified with the Bemba as well as the Movement for Multi-Party Democracy (MMD) albeit less conspicuous after the second president's departure and court cases.

The formation of political parties based on ethnic foundations is practically institutionalised in this way. Once a party comes into power, almost all presidential appointments to public office are given to people who come from the same clan, village or neighbouring village and ultimately from the same ethnic grouping. This is known as the ethnicisation of public institutions. The

Third president of Zambia has been criticized more for creating what the public came to call the "Mwanawasa Family Tree." It is a tree diagram of the strong family relationships between the president and his appointees, including those that came from other parties. Almost all the evidence on the appointments revealed a family tie. One appointee or the other is from the Lenje ethnic group, the president's ethnicity.

In African public institutions such as the government ministries, the police and others, it is likely that one employee or the other will trace his engagement to someone they know and ultimately leading to someone who knows the president. People are mostly employed on the basis of who you know that works there, who in turn knows the minister, who knows… who is the president's relative. This system of appointments developed during the early post-independence years when appointments were made with regard to the contribution one made to the independence struggle regardless of academic qualifications. The injustice is that employment on merit has been compromised. It is based on patronage through ethnic links, to the exclusion of people from other ethnic groupings that may, in most instances, be more suitable for the positions. It further goes to the extent that government contracts are awarded to businesses of fellow tribesmen.

Kenya is another case in point. Parties that still had aspired to a national, multi-ethnic support base at the time of the 1992 elections participated in the 1997 elections as ethnic parties.[21] When such parties come into power, they share political and civil service positions on ethnic considerations.

The description I have given above is an objective description of African ethnicity and it's permeation into every aspect of society. Ethnicity has already affected the process of development and nation building in Africa for over half a decade. As Africans struggle to survive in the economic system that holds globalisation together, ethnicity poses a threat too dangerous to ignore.

Girma Yilma Bulbula[22], former Ambassador of Ethiopia to the Soviet Union stated thus;

> The problem with many Africans… is that we have accepted and internalized this colonialist notion that ethnicism, in one or another form, gives us our identity as citizens, or Africans. It is this self-conception which has nothing to do with the real African history, which constitutes the main hindrance to meaningful national economic, political, and social development.

> Ethnic nationalism should be condemned and fought in Africa. As long as it thrives, there will be little prospect for achieving the political stability and focus needed for rapid economic development and nation-building. There will be very little opportunity for Africa to survive globalization. Ethnic nationalism is a destructive force that breeds intolerance and parochialism, much in the same way as racial nationalism. It is odd that there exists universal liberal consensus on the evil of racism, but ethnicism, which has caused the deaths of millions of people in Africa and elsewhere, is not so viewed. The ethnic warlords who stirred hatred that caused civil wars in different parts of Africa are as evil as were German Nazis... Ethnicism and racism share many common features, including defining a set of people in counter-distinction to other groups and

blaming others for problems, particularly economic under-achievement.

Globalisation as the interaction of different cultures could help broaden people's minds and encourage them to view themselves as members of a heterogeneous global community. Without denying obvious differences in their ethnic, racial or sexual roots, people need to learn that their prime identity is as individual members of the human race. Ethnicity, race or sex need not determine where one lives or works, whom one marries or befriends, or one's faith and loyalties. This broadening of self- consciousness can be liberating and will lessen the potential for social conflict.

Chapter Three

Globalisation

Defining Globalization

Among my contemporaries, I found that globalisation has had a tremendous impact on our lives, not only in terms of opportunities but also in terms of negative consequences. Yet many tell me that they have little or no idea what globalisation is. In this chapter, I comprehensively deal with Globalisation from the point of view of its existence before the 1920s, through the establishment of the Bretton Woods institutions to the coining of the term "Washington Consensus" by John Williamson in 1989[23].

Globalisation is mainly an economic process technically traced to the first family on earth. If we take Adam and Eve, their first step out of Eden was the first step towards globalisation. Adam and his wife ventured into new lands in order to survive by engaging in production and consumption of food, shelter, clothing etc. Centuries later, during the 14th century Renaissance, that step out of Eden had developed to voyages on the oceans of the great planet finding new lands on which they could engage in production and higher quality consumption. By the seventeenth and eighteenth centuries, the Industrial Revolution caused the movement of labour from Africa to Europe and the Americas. This was an early form of internationalization of labour for production. It goes without mentioning that production capital was already internationalized within Europe when cotton was being imported from France by the British. At the same time, textile machines were being exported to other countries. By 1929, just before the Great Depression, trade between countries, kingdoms and continents had increased to global proportions. However, the protectionism that ensued slowed down the rate of globalization for the next one and half decades.

Learning from the depression, John Maynard Keynes, one of the most influential economists from the United Kingdom and Henry Dexter White of the United States envisioned a world in which countries envisaged a common commitment to practical and constructive internationalism through the creation of a new universal economic system ruled by law. This intergovernmental commitment would facilitate the creation of a system in which governments could establish a stable global economic system, with universal international monetary policies that all nations could agree upon.

Thus, the two scholars became influential founding fathers of the agreement of Bretton Woods. The Bretton Woods Conference held from July 1 to 22, 1944 in New Hampshire USA brought nations together to create institutions that would address the changing needs of the post- World War Two global economy. The result was the World Bank, International Monetary Fund and The General Agreement on Tariffs and Trade (GATT) in 1995 changed to The World Trade Organization. The foundation for globalization as it has come to be known in the twentieth century was therefore laid.

The Washington Consensus

During the 1990s, the world was under the impression that there was a clear and robust consensus about what poor countries of Africa should do to become more prosperous[24]. This misimpression clearly owed a lot to the emerging popularity of the term "Washington Consensus," the name that economist John Williamson gave in 1989 to a list of ten policy recommendations for countries willing to reform their economies.

The phrase "Washington Consensus" is often used synonymously with "neo-liberalism" and "globalization" policies that have been imposed on African and other developing countries by the Washington-based international financial institutions. The Washington Consensus was named so, and consists of a set of economic policies endorsed, by the Washington Based U.S. Treasury, the Federal Reserve Board, International Monetary Fund and World Bank. These policies more comprehensively encapsulate the definition of globalization.

Naim asserts that Williamson originally coined the phrase Washington Consensus in 1989 "to refer to the lowest common denominator of policy advice given by the Washington-based institutions [IMF, World Bank] to Latin American countries as of 1989." These policies were fiscal discipline, a redirection of public expenditure priorities toward fields offering both high economic returns and the potential to improve income distribution, such as primary health care, basic education, and infrastructure, tax reform, Interest rate liberalization, a competitive exchange rate and Trade liberalization, liberalization of inflows of foreign direct investment, privatization and deregulation (to abolish barriers to entry and exit), and secure property rights. The policies soon became pre conditions for multilateral and bilateral aid giving and were the essence of the Structural Adjustment Programmes.

The term 'Washington Consensus' is often used interchangeably with the phrase "neo-liberal policies."

Clearly, the definition of the term has been subjected to various interpretations by Williamson and other economists. Naim, (ibid) has further argued that no such consensus exists. Though the various economists and Naim argue in those lines, the fulcrum of the matter is that the package of structural adjustment was composed of the above policies. Some policy discussion, however, might still be understood by using the term as a reference point. The term "Washington Consensus" came to be used to describe an extreme and dogmatic commitment to the belief that markets can handle everything in the lives of individuals. This is commonly referred to as politics of market fundamentalisn."

The timing of the formulation of the Washington Consensus coincided with the sudden collapse of the Socialist system. The world-weariness with socialist ideas and central planning, which had pervaded many developing countries outside the Soviet block, created an urgent and widespread need for an alternative set of ideas about how to organize economic and political life.

Backed by the successful policies of Reaganomics and Thatcherism (belief in free trade and privatization respectively), the Washington Consensus became an all-encompassing ideological framework on which millions of people had come to depend to guide their opinions about economic affairs, judge public policies and even to steer some aspects of their daily lives.

The developed countries through the IMF and the World Bank made their loans conditional on the adoption of Washington Consensus-inspired policy reforms by now called SAP. This inevitably set aid-seeking African countries on a path to implementing the policies as IMF and World Bank conditions for receiving aid.

Main Players in Globalisation
The main players in the process of globalization have been increasing since the conference of Bretton Woods. In 1944, the main players were the governments of developed countries with the leadership of the United States of America. In the twenty first century, each government is a player. However, the number of governments that joined the IMF, World Bank and WTO increased rapidly a decade after the conference following decolonisation. Through these organisations and as its own entity, the United Nations is a principle player in globalisation. There are also private sector players which are by far the most visible to my contemporaries. A few

of us call them private investors while by Bemba language pronunciation, they are called private infesters.

The multilateral institutions (IMF, World Bank and WTO) are a central set of players whose primary purpose is to ensure that the rules of globalization are enacted and enforced by member governments. However, unequal terms characterise the conditions under which these rules are made and enforced. The typical example is that of the IMF in which the United States of America is the only country with veto power. In addition, agreements to equalise the world trade regime for developing countries reached during the Doha trade rounds of talks and the Uruguay Round were not implemented by the developed countries while the African and other developing countries implemented them. This substantially contributed to the breakdown of the Seattle and Cancun talks.

The primary players in the process of globalization are the Multinational Corporations (MNCs). The conditions created by globalization or Washington Consensus policies are good for their business. Diverse economic, technological, political and cultural principles and subsystems in trade between nations make business difficult.

Mechanisms of Globalisation
Internationalization of Production
The primary pillar of globalisation is economic production of commodity goods and services. For commodities from any country to be incorporated in the process of globalisation, they must enter the international market. The underlying assumption in this process is

that producers produce enough goods and services to satisfy the demand of the local market first. Then those commodities produced in surplus are set to meet the demand of the global market. However, it is not as simple as that and not always the case. Some goods, specifically cash crops of developing countries are produced solely for the international market causing a shortage of food and an increase in prices on the local market.

In addition, surplus production for the international market brings in issues of value-added on goods and services to meet the high international standards.

Globalisation is not just about producing goods locally. It derives its purpose from the internationalisation of the process of production itself. For a company to maximise profits, it must pay the lowest possible costs on labour, machinery and raw materials. At the same time it must sale the produce at the most profitable price. To lower production costs, globalisation has made it possible for companies to source their cheap labour from countries like Asia, their raw materials from all over Africa, and their machinery from industrialised countries of Europe and America. Then they are able to find ready market and high demand at a profitable price in Africa, Latin America and Asia. At the crux of globalisation of production are the Multinational Corporations (MNCs). A Multinational Corporation is a firm of a particular nationality that has organized its production processes across national boundaries.

Gilpin[25] defines an MNC as "a firm of a particular nationality with partly or wholly owned subsidiaries with two or more national economies. Such firms expand overseas primarily through Foreign Direct Investment."

In more detail, the process of global economic integration involves the increase in foreign investment. Recent trends have shown that MNCs are increasingly investing across national borders and continents and building their stocks all over the world. In fact, Gilpin asserts that the term globalization came into popular usage in the second half of the 1980s in connection with the huge surge in FDI by MNCs

Foreign Direct Investment allows MNCs to establish subsidiaries in other countries other than their own in order to reduce costs. The costs of labour and raw materials are high in developed countries as compared to Africa, Asia and Latin America

The movement of finance and equipment as capital is facilitated by the Washington Consensus policies. The policies provide a free market environment. This helps ensure the maximization of production as costs of transportation of capital, and tax are circumvented.

global corporate mergers and alliances emerged as catalysts in the process of globalization at the close of the twentieth century.. The benefits are attractive. In the midst of competition for the global market, there is not a bigger alternative to profit maximization than corporate merging

Sub Saharan Africa's participation in globalisation has been insignificant. Foreign Direct Investment is concentrated among the developed countries. The benefits continue to accrue Westward while in Africa, we have continued on the path to Marginalisation. Gilpin observes that despite much talk of corporate globalization, Foreign Direct Investment is actually highly concentrated and distributed very unevenly around the globe. Most FDI takes place in and among the United States, China, European Union and Japan because firms are attracted to large or partially large markets. As for Africa, FDI is generally a one directional activity in which the developed countries invest in Africa. At the same time, the developed countries have tightened up their markets to investors coming from Africa except for some large South African MNCs. The fact continues to be that Africa is still being used as a source of cheap raw materials and as a market for goods coming from the developed countries albeit in new ways.

Foreign Direct Investment has further been concentrated in capital intensive sectors. This has been to the contrary of the interests of African countries because their economies are labour intensive. Much labour has been marginalized from economic activities and consequently from a source of livelihood.

Privatization
In all Sub Saharan countries that implemented SAP, the privatization of key sectors and strategic firms and industries attracted FDI. Parastatal firms found in the banking, telecommunication and electricity supply sectors have been the targets. Other targets include the mining sector that plays the role of an economic backbone in Zambia. Multinational Corporations therefore globalize

their activities by taking advantage of the privatization policies pursued under SAP.

These policies have mainly been unsuccessful simply because privatization policies in Sub Saharan Africa were not an African initiative. Though portrayed as country initiatives, they are of the IMF and World Bank. In this regard, it can be observed that the IMF, World Bank and WTO are complimenting each other's work in the formation of globalisation.

The World Trade Organization is working toward the removal of tariff and non-tariff barriers to trade in order to enable international firms easily invest through FDI. The IMF has practically imposed SAP without humanitarian consideration. The World Bank on the other hand is more focussed on poverty reduction but still imposes SAP as conditions for its aid giving. For example, the IMF may give aid on the condition that a country privatizes a major industry or parastatal firm. This indirectly guarantees profits to MNCs because of investment in economically viable sectors. This is compounded by the fact that indigenous Africans are hardly able to invest because of capital deficiency.

The effects of privatization in Sub Saharan Africa were economically destructive. Africa was stripped of its capital base as local firms and industries fell into foreign hands. Structural Adjustment disabled Sub Saharan Africa's capacity to create wealth independently because all the countries' assets fell into foreign hands. The wealth created in Sub Saharan Africa today goes to MNC headquarters in form of capital flight.

Companies in developed countries had the financial capital and opportunities under SAP to invest in Africa, as opposed to Sub Saharan Africans. The developed countries have not provided the opportunity for the continent's foreign investors to invest in North America and Europe. Neither have the governments provided their markets for African businessmen to sell their products as per WTO regulations.

International Trade

The system of international trade makes it possible for globalization to occur, that is, for countries to be able to buy and sell their commodities on the international market. The argument in most economics texts is that developing countries have not been growing because they have not embraced free trade by breaking down protectionist policies such as import substitution industrialization (ISI) strategy and generally breaking down tariff and non-tariff barriers to trade. A free international trading system must be efficient allowing the flow of goods and services from one place to another. However, our societies in Sub Saharan Africa and Zambia in particular have a major problem of low quantity and low quality productivity. Hence their participation in international trade hit the first self-built brick wall.

The late 1970s and early 1980s witnessed a rise in protectionist measures in a number of countries. During the same period, Japan "was pursuing what business consultant Peter Drucker characterized as "adversarial" trade policies. It exported manufactured goods but did not import them from non Japanese producers."[26]

This apparently caused a response from American Congressmen who put pressure on the Reagan Administration for trade protection because of the persistence of the huge annual trade deficits.

In Africa, this period is associated with the springing up of the one-party system whose policies were those of Nationalization. The parastatal firms that emerged were considered infant and needed to be protected until they could survive the competition from the international firms. Import substitution measures and import and export taxes were the most common barriers tariff barriers against imports. Others included quota allocations and state subsidies.

Protectionist policies were also the consequence of the global rise in oil prices and the fall in commodity prices on the international market. The driving force behind protectionism is the nationalistic tendency to keep trade within national boundaries. Keeping trade within national boundaries implies that some of the countries will not sale as much and hence reduce its buying power of imported goods. This implies that the other countries from which it imports goods will also have a reduced income. This chain reaction continues and causes a global economic recession. This is what happened during the depression in 1929 and the recession in Asia in the 1990s.

Coming from this background, Africa in the twenty first century is in protectionism inertia and has a challenge to pursue liberal policies, albeit cautiously due to distortions in the international trade system.

However, the effect of parastatal companies that continues to haunt Sub Saharan Africa is the reduction in productivity because of the lack of competition that obtained prior to structural adjustment programmes.

Global Finance

In international trade, the instruments of transaction between firms from different countries begin with national currencies. The movement of financial capital and capital in form of equipment in the process of FDI is accompanied by the movement of credit finance usually in American dollars, deposited in financial institutions-banks. The US dollar is the major currency used in international trade. African currencies in the twenty first century continue to be at a disadvantage in their balance of payments because in order for them to participate in international trade, they have to convert their currencies into the dollar. This is an added because inflation is high. Therefore we need much more African currency (in many cases over a thousand) to buy US $1.00. This implies that Sub Saharan African countries buy less quantity due to lower power parity. It also means their revenue is less because production is done under local currencies.

Rapid Development in Information and Communication Technology

Since the beginning of time, man has never experienced a faster increase in information and communication technology as that of the twenty-first century. Today, information is only a click of a button away. There is an information and technological revolution. World travel is increasing at unprecedented cheaper rates. Because of the Internet, more people are able to send instant messages through electronic mail. People can use essential gadgets like cellular phones to talk to each other from any part of the world and may even look at each other through videophone. We are able to communicate and exchange ideas in an instant today what we could communicate in a year half a century ago.

As a result, rapid global integration of the worlds' peoples is taking place. Chat rooms on the Internet have provided platforms on which people from all parts of the world exchange ideas about matters affecting them as though they were in the same room. It is as though people from the whole world are at a village chatting and this is the global village.

Because of international travel, people from different nations and backgrounds are able to interact at airports, train stations, docking areas, bus stations and cruise ships. International travel has become more varied and affordable. Therefore, people are meeting more frequently.

Globalisation is the movement toward global uniformity, the harmonising of a multiplicity of subsystems and cultures into the modern world; the western culture. Thus the result has been the emergence of a global culture of tolerance for other people's beliefs, ideas and cultures. This culture is called multiculturalism.

The media is playing a critical role in the globalization of social life. Today, people of different backgrounds are watching television programmes of numerous nations other than their own.

The pattern of cultural change in the not so distant future will be seen to converge to a common point at which all peoples of the world will meet with little disagreements. It is most likely to be science and logic-based, a culture of universalism. This means that the world will continue to head toward secularism upon which western countries are based.

As a result, people have realized the need of having at least one second language because of the increase in multilingual, multicultural and international social interaction. This will be vital for Sub Saharan Africa. In addition, MNCs and other international organizations, as they increase their scope of operation, are demanding more multicultural oriented employees.

Political Globalization
After the September 11, 2001 terrorist attacks in New York and Washington DC, the global political arena has rapidly integrated. Nations have been united in the fight against terrorism and many other issues, speaking a common voice. Statesmen have visibly increased interaction and cooperation.

It can be postulated that globalization will have its final destiny, the creation of a global government. The creation of a global government will be the total eradication of Nationalism and localism. The current process of political globalization will finally result in a global system of government, a global constitution, and a global leadership. This will be the greatest challenge democracy will ever face. Currently, the United Nations is the closest system we have to global government.

Today, globalization is irreversible and will continue moving ahead until the world leaders develop a tangible political framework of one worldism through the establishment, under the law of a global government.

Indeed for most Sub Saharan African countries, globalization is not voluntary as the countries did not choose to be part of the process simply because they did not have much of a choice.

Globalisation and Production

The fulcrum of globalisation, from which all issues discussed above emanate, is simply production. The basic argument therefore that everyone of us in Zambia and the Sub Saharan African region in general must know after this discourse is that our hope to survive and thrive in the Twenty First Century lies in producing enough goods and services to meet the needs of our local economies and to produce a surplus in order to meet the demand of the international market. Globalisation is basically a production system of the Twenty First Century. It is about how productive I am as an individual, and how productive we are as a nation and as a global economy. The underlying assumption here is that surplus production attracts market and creates innovation in the production and marketing of goods and services. It creates jobs and more jobs for us and helps our economies grow.

I suggest here that globalisation goes with a particular culture or value of surplus production and not subsistence production. Globalisation demands a culture of the production of the more than enough for our country and not the production of the enough.

There is dire need for the acquisition and employment of latest technology in form of knowledge, equipment and high-tech to increase production of goods and services in order for any country to survive and thrive in the Twenty First Century.

Chapter Four

Multinational Corporations (MNCs) in Africa in the Twenty First Century

During the late 80s, we did not see that many advertisements, whether on TV, or in the streets. The only decorations we would see in the streets were usually the national flag colours displayed along Independence Avenue during independence celebrations. Companies and their products had either the word "Zambia" or "National" added to their name; Zambia Breweries, United Bus Company of Zambia, Zambia Consolidated Copper Mines, National Milling and the like. Almost each company was either partly or wholly-owned by the government. We were a proud nation to have all these industries to our name. Back in the colonial days, all companies were privately owned by the colonial masters, most notably the British-South Africa Company (BSA Company). I am reliably informed that it was such a horrible experience, being ruled by racist, oppressive and imperialist businessmen from Great Britain. Independence Day (October 24, 1964) was therefore truly liberating. It is no wonder that a few years after independence, the President of Zambia announced what he termed "The Mulungushi Reforms", a series of decisions to nationalise the country's major industries and empower Zambians. However, the 1990s saw the return of privatisation and the Multinational Corporations. They possess the required production culture needed for any country to survive globalisation.

In the 1990s, they bought assets of businesses undergoing the process of privatisation in Sub Saharan countries. In 2001, MNCs from the United States invested over US $I billion in the Sub-Saharan African region.

The policies of globalisation from the international financial institutions are primarily implemented by MNCs. The Washington Consensus Policies are good for the business of the MNC. This is because diverse economic principles, ideologies and economic systems makes business difficult hence they push the process of globalisation in order to make business easier. In fact, the relationship between the IMF and MNCs is a healthy one. As Stiglitz[27] put it

> "…many of its [the IMF] key personnel came from the financial community. Stan Fischer [born in Ndola, Zambia], the Deputy Managing Director who played such a role in the episodes described in this book, went directly from the IMF to become a vice president at Citigroup, the vast financial firm [multinational] that includes Citibank. A chairman of Citigroup (chairman of the executive committee) was Robert Rubin, who, as Secretary of Treasury [US equivalent of Minister of Finance] had had a central role in IMF policies. One could only ask, was Fischer being richly rewarded for having faithfully executed what he was told to do?"

The MNCs push for favourable global economic conditions at the IMF for them to smoothly conduct global business. In their countries of origin, they have influence especially through political contributions. They influence domestic policy by supporting political parties that push policies that they want on the international scene. They even employ full-time lobbyists for the government to implement the policies that they want. They influence foreign policy in that the MNCs come from countries whose governments are major shareholders in the World Bank and IMF. Therefore they influence the international multilateral institutions through interest articulation to their governments.

Walter Rodney[28] argued that in the 1970s, for every US $I invested in Africa, US $5 were reaped as profits and sent back to the investing country. Investment figures alone portray an increase in a country's capital and therefore economic growth. On a large scale, foreign investment is repeatedly argued for as the fastest path to economic growth because it portrays high rates of GDP and GNP growth. However, this is only for the while before funds are wired to the headquarters.

The case in Zambia and indeed Sub Saharan Africa is that the profits are not re-invested. Profits are repatriated to the headquarters of the MNC. Multinational Corporations are instruments of African economic resource transfer to the developed countries. The World Investment Directory 1996[29] shows evidence that billions of dollars were invested in Sub Saharan Africa between 1970 and 1996. Generally, little or no re-investment took place. What happened to the profits? In 2002, Anglo American

Corporation had decided to withdraw its investment from Zambia in order to invest in a mine in Chile. Anglo American Corporation had invested US $56 million and made profits of over US $400 million. This was Zambian money leaving while the nation watched. That is where the money goes, back home to the headquarters in order to be channelled to other uses while the host country loses out.

The World Investment Report also revealed that between 1970 and 1996 little or no FDI flows took place from Africa to the outside regions, particularly to the developed countries. This trend is still the scenario today. We need our firms to be able to invest abroad and do the same elsewhere because if we do not, our countries in Sub Saharan Africa will not survive globalisation. In addition, it is stark reality that these are the rules of the game in globalisation.

Multinational Corporations have been found to manipulate the political, economic and administrative systems to maximize profits because of the unchecked, uncontrolled and unregulated freedom given to them.

Cutting down Production Costs

Apart from labour costs, there are also environmental protection costs where companies must produce in such a way that they do not harm the environment. Therefore, to cut down production costs, some MNCs engage in unorthodox strategies that violate labour regulations.

Firstly, some MNCs pay minimum wages that are sometimes lower than the income required for one to make a living. They have taken advantage of the high unemployment situation in Africa. Africa has abundant supply on its labour market. As a result, MNCs pay low wages to African employees knowing that if he or she strikes, he or she can readily be replaced. This deprives most African employees of their right to strike. The individual is disadvantaged in terms of negotiation. Government departments looking into labour laws and standards are disregarded because of the assertion that they need investment so if the investors are subjected to enough regulation, they will pull out. In some cases, investors do threaten to pull out. If the wages of the Africans working for MNCs are compared to those in subsidiaries operating in the developed countries in similar capacities, Africans are paid about 40 times lower. A blue collar job fetches US $15 per week (US $2,400 per month) in New York while it fetches US $63 per month in Africa

Secondly, MNCs in Africa tend to keep employees on probation for abnormally long periods of time. During probation, the salary or wages are termed temporary and are low. In some instances, employees have gone without confirmation for over two years. After that, some have been relinquished of their jobs for others to be hired and to undergo the same conditions.

Thirdly, MNCs tend to create positions in and actually employ unskilled or manual labour from their hosts in African countries and very few white-collar employees. As Max Weber argued, the value of an individual on the labour market is determined by the qualifications, competence and skills he or she possesses. Unskilled and semi skilled labour is not certainly expensive. Yet in some cases, the workload and responsibilities given to such employees is much higher than their job specifications and descriptions and the pay is much lower than they deserve. The investors and the people they come with from their countries normally occupy the few executive positions.

In addition, MNCs frequently employ women in order to cut costs. Women are generally paid lower than men are, if compared under the same capacities. It is therefore an advantage to utilize women in the labour force to lower production costs and maximize profits.

Fourthly, MNCs evade taxes charged by the host country to reduce costs of production[30]. When negotiating their investment deals with governments, they demand for tax-free investment deals such as tax holidays and or other tax privileges. In the case of Anglo American Corporation described above, the MNC demanded for a tax holiday for the first five years of operations then begin to remit after that. Immediately after the five years elapsed and the firm had made its profits, it pulled out.

In certain industries, MNCs are monopolies especially when they come to Africa. Manufacturing sectors like automobile manufacturing and information and communication technology sectors are obvious monopolies from the developed countries. They are sectors responsible for the supply of capital goods. Many academics claim that they are instruments of technological transfer. However, capital products are extremely expensive for Africa. One cannot help but wonder whether the commodities are actually at the correct price or deliberately set to be too expensive for the Africans. This is because capital goods will enable Africa extract and process its raw materials into finished manufactured goods to enable it compete with those from the developed countries.

Africa can rise as a powerful competitor in the global economy if it had access to mass production capital goods. Scholars, writers, politicians and statesmen have said time and again that Africa is a sleeping giant. However, few have said why. Therefore, MNCs price capital goods too high for Africa. In addition, patent rights managed and regulated through the World Intellectual Property Organization (WIPO) hinder African access to technology and other capital goods. One can hardly understand the practicality of the argument that MNCs are instruments of technology transfer.

If the world wants to see Africa survive globalisation in the twenty first century, Africa must be accorded adequate access to technology and capital goods so that it sets up its own manufacturing sector and compete with the MNCs from the developed countries.

MNCs create employment in the host country though and this is a plus. Even a low wage makes a difference as compared to nothing at all.

Chapter Five

International Financial Institutions and Africa in the Twenty First Century

The Bretton Woods Institutions

It was the winter of 1997. I remember the complaints about the rising unemployment rates extending from school leavers to University graduates. I recollect the low wages and the famous wage freeze for all civil servants, who constitute the highest number of people in formal employment in Zambia. Soldiers expressed discontent that their country was being run unsatisfactorily. They staged a failed coup attempt that has come to be known as the Captain Solo Coup. There was also an eruption of severely destructive riots at boarding schools all over the country, one occurring at the school I was. In the same vein, the University of Zambia was closed. Some of these events were fatal. It was a time when the implementation of SAP was in its crucial season. No one seemed to see the real connection between these independent events though. But in each case, everybody blamed the Fredrick Chiluba led government for its poor policies. However, there was a more present yet invisible force behind these incidences; the policies of the Bretton Woods Institutions, which in other words can be summed up as a country's pre-requisite to global integration.

The IMF and World Bank both originated in World War II as a result of the United Nations Monetary and Financial Conference held at Bretton Woods, New Hampshire, in July 1944. It was part of a concerted effort to finance the rebuilding of Europe after the devastation of the war and to save the world from future economic depressions[31]. The International Monetary Fund was assigned the task of ensuring global economic stability and to prevent another global depression. According to Stiglitz, "it would do this by putting international pressure on countries that were not doing their fair share to maintain global aggregate demand, by allowing their own economies to go into a slump".

[32]The World Bank was first known as the International Bank for Reconstruction and Development. It was established to rebuild Europe from the devastating effects of the war. Stiglitz adds that the "last part, "Development", was added almost as an afterthought. At the time, most of the countries in the developing world were still colonies, and what meagre economic development efforts could or would be undertaken were considered the responsibility of their European masters." This must give us the most important lesson for Zambia and the rest of Sub Saharan Africa in relation to the IMF and the World Bank; that in the original plan, we were not part of the economic community of nations.

The depression visibly affected Europe and the United States. Those who convened at Bretton Woods had the experience constantly on their minds. The lessons were fresh, having seen the devastating and fatal consequences of the recession. They therefore put in place these institutions to guard against the recurrence of economic catastrophes in the Americas and to reconstruct Europe.

These multilateral financial institutions were charged with the role to lend money and borrow money internationally to and from institutions, governments and companies in nation states. They borrow from rich nations and rich international companies. Because of their international nature, they are also mandated with the creation of money by issuing out bonds. A bond is technically a loan which when given out generates immediate cash to the borrower (usually our governments or international banks) for use on structural adjustment and poverty reduction programmes. As issuers, the international financial institutions get interest on the loans. The institutions do not only accrue interest on the international bonds. They go out of there way to impose conditions and purposes in and for which the funds a government borrows must be utilised. Our governments were given funds on the basis that they implement the Structural Adjustment Programmes we experienced in the 1990s.

Africa and The Structural Adjustment Programs
In 1981, the government of Mexico announced that it was unable to repay its debt of over US $110 billion. The creditor nations that lend to the IMF and World Bank and the international financial institutions themselves were alarmed. They began to seek arrangements through which they would help the Mexican government repay its

debt without causing harm to both the Mexican economy and the global economy. Soon, other Latin American countries including from Africa followed the Mexican example by defaulting to pay back loans. The debts the governments had accrued were unsustainable.

With the leadership and control of the United States, the then president Ronald Reagan worked through the United States Treasury with the IMF and World Bank to formulate SAP. Structural Adjustment Programs were supposed to overhaul and transform defaulting nations permanently, thereby overcoming structural rigidities in their economies. The structural rigidities were identified to have been caused by government involvement in the economy and all aspects of life of its citizenry. Therefore, economic capital had to change hands from government to the private sector and the government's role was to be significantly reduced.

For over twenty years now, Structural Adjustment Programmes have been implemented as IMF and World Bank conditionality for aid giving in Sub Saharan Africa. Conditionality refers to the conditions that international lenders imposed in return for their assistance that undermined national sovereignty[33] and economic self determination. It is obvious that a nation that has announced default of debt repayment is in dire need of funding. Its government would do anything desperate to get funds. On this understanding, the IMF and World Bank imposed SAP as conditions upon which to lend.

The claim by the IMF and World Bank that each country implementing SAP decided on its own through the Policy Framework Paper (PFP) is unfounded. Stiglitz describes a scene that brings out the true picture the IMF cautiously hides;

> ...the IMF is not particularly interested in hearing the thoughts of its "client countries" on such topics as development strategy or fiscal austerity. All too often, the fund's approach to developing countries has had the feel of a colonial ruler. A picture can be worth a thousand words, and a single picture snapped in 1998, shown throughout the world, has engraved itself in the minds of millions, particularly those in the former colonies. The IMF's Managing Director (the head of the IMF is referred to as "Managing Director"), a short, neatly dressed former French Treasury bureaucrat, who once claimed to be a Socialist, is standing with a stern face and crossed arms over the seated and humiliated president of Indonesia. The hapless president was being forced, in effect, to turn over economic sovereignty of his country to the IMF in return for the aid his country needed... (Officially, the "ceremony" was the signing of a letter of agreement, an agreement effectively dictated by the IMF, though it often still keeps up the pretence that the letter comes from the country's government!).

This picture confirms the imposition of conditionalities that the IMF has so often openly denied. In this case, one major question we must ask ourselves is 'who runs our country in Zambia and countries in Sub Saharan Africa? And with the devastating effects of the policies pursued under SAP, does the IMF care whether we live or not? In answering this question, my answers to both questions are partly positive but mostly negative, based on the facts and my personal experiences growing up in the 1990s, and I think I speak on behalf of many.

Structural Adjustment Programmes have five main goals or components. They are trade liberalization, macro-economic stabilization, privatization of public enterprises, public sector reform and good governance, basically Washington Consensus policies described in chapter two.

The United States Treasury Department, the IMF and World Bank in their publications generally argue that these policies will enable a country service its debt, efficiently and effectively use its resources for production yet they ignore the social consequences to the Zambian and African on the streets.

What trade liberalization has done is to create competition between MNCs and local firms. In Zambia, local firms have either been displaced or shut down because they could not withstand the competition. In addition, because of the high costs of production that result from high electricity tariffs, transport and telecommunication costs and generally capital expenditure, African firms were forced to sell their commodities at higher prices in order to make profits. Therefore, they are unable to compete with the cheaper, higher quality commodities from MNCs. Consequently, local firms and industries have been forced out of competition leading to trade monopoly on the local market.

With the emergence of trade monopolies from abroad, Africa is an emerging chronic importer of the majority of its goods and services for consumption and will be for a long time to come.

In this regard, the trade pattern is unfair to Africa. It is one directional trade. Most African countries import while the developed countries export to Africa. One can agree that the developed countries, the IMF and the World Bank have perpetuated the pattern of trade that obtained under colonialism. No doubt we as Africans have also contributed because of our low levels of production.

For many African nations, the revenue base has been narrowed as a consequence of privatization. While our governments are able to get tax from the foreign firms, they do this after a foreign firm has had a tax holidays of up to five years before paying its' first tax. Sometimes the firm closes down its offices after this period and comes back in another name in order to enjoy more of this privilege. In Zambia, the 2006 budget showed that corporate tax contributed only a meagre K2 billion to Zambia's GDP while pay as you earn and other taxes on ordinary Zambian citizens catered for a significant portion of GDP, K44 billion.

It is sad that Zambians carry more of the tax burden than corporate bodies. It will be worse with the IMF proposed tax on food which is already costly on the Zambian families. National income from ordinary citizens is not enough to carry out the majority of Zambia's development programmes. Because of tax holidays and low contribution of corporate tax to the budget, the option that continues to be present is further bilateral borrowing from the wealthy countries, and multilateral borrowing from the IMF and World Bank, which continues, even with debt write-offs, to delve the countries further into debt and external control.

The experience of the 1990s with MNCs in Africa showed that they often reduce both the workforce and wages once they purchase the public enterprise, in an effort to reduce production costs. Subsequently, unemployment rates increased. The large organization sizes of the public enterprises in Africa were in a number of cases a political strategy to keep unemployment levels low and in turn poverty levels low. This was a social welfare strategy in which people are encouraged to work for what they earn in order for them to make a living.

Macro-economic stabilization policies under SAP include fiscal discipline, monetary policy, budget control, exchange rate policy, inflation rate and the interest rate policies. Fiscal discipline emphasizes the fact that government must spend what it makes. This means that government expenditure must be less than or equal to government revenue. Monetary control emphasizes a minimum supply of money in circulation and reduced amount of public credit and loans in order to control inflation. By far, the most important figure that the IMF concentrates on, above all else is the inflation rate. It is the first thing they look at when analysing a country's economic performance.

Budget control emphasizes the importance of governments sticking as closely as they possibly can to their budgets. The moment any African country violates loses budget control, the IMF demands an explanation. This is also a mechanism to ensure debt resettlement. It is called the cash budget. The IMF and the World Bank monitor a country's debt servicing and priorities of expenditure. Exchange rate policies demand the floating of the currency of a country so that it reflects its real value. This came as a reaction to the tendency of fixing exchange rates that most countries had. Its common method is devaluation and revaluation of the currency. For Africa, revaluation has been impossible since SAP. Finally, the freeing of interest rates implies that the market decides the cost at which money should be borrowed and not those fixed by the state, especially in accessing loans and other forms of credit.

Among SAP implementing countries, Uganda, Rwanda, Botswana, Namibia and Mozambique had less negative effects. However, since SAP's first implementation in the region in the 1980s, "Sub-Saharan Africa's debt has increased by nearly 400 per cent"[34]. There has been reduced government expenditure on health and agriculture as a result of reduced levels of money in circulation and the cash budget. Subsidies have been reduced or totally eradicated virtually throwing millions into poverty and squalor. Debt servicing is also increasingly squeezing as much as it possibly can from the already meagre financial resources in African coffers leaving little or no funds for development purposes.

The early 1990s saw the abandoning of fixed exchange rates (except in the EU) and embracing flexible exchange rates, a disaster for most African countries. Time and again, countries in Africa devalue their currencies. The implication is that the import of commodities from other countries outside the African region is increasingly expensive and that countries from other regions of the world import African commodities at a cheaper price. The sector most affected is health, where anti-retroviral drugs for the approximately 35 million HIV/AIDS infected people are too expensive or even impossible to purchase even for the government. By 2006 in Zambia, about 72 000 people were on anti-retroviral therapy (CSO Selected Socio-Economic Indicators).

Public sector reforms by far were and continue to be a great source of trepidation in the public sector. In most instances, the aim of public sector reform policies were to downsize the over-staffed civil service and the number of public institutions primarily to reduce public expenditure. This is why a short time after implementation of SAPs, unemployment rises.

As a result, there were massive retrenchments and retirements in the public service coupled with the liquidation of public enterprises. This threw the majority of Zambians into destitution, with no means of earning a livelihood. In Africa, public sector employment is the second most reliable means of earning a living after subsistence farming. It is also worth recalling that many African states were socialist oriented, a system in which all employees of the country were government employees. Therefore there was massive scaling down and massive social dislocation.

After such job-cuts, a few unemployed people have been able to venture into and survive the foreign dominated private sector. For most, the pensions and benefits they get are of little value because of devaluation, the lack of interest accumulation and late payments as interacting factors.

Perhaps, the policy recommendation of universal acceptance among SAP is good governance. It aims at enhancing transparency and accountability in our corruption infested countries. Though not addressing the cultural root cause, it is a major policy for the reduction of corruption. Undoubtedly, the best means to implement such a policy is through democratization. Africa has increasingly embraced democracy in the twenty-first century. It has been a worthy cause. However, some countries still possess authoritarian traits as a result of the historical and cultural orientations.

The weakness inherent in African democracy is that it is imposed from the outside. It has been a result of pressure from the developed countries, IMF, World Bank and the United Nations. Actually, democratization is also part of conditionality for aid giving by the major donors. It has not come as a result of African values. The majority of the population does not know what kind of political system is being used to rule them. A government may claim to be democratic and even practice it, but the people at the grassroots do not understand the democratic system. All they know is that their leaders will sort out their problems and just issue commands without their participation.

Structural Adjustment Programs were the source of economic reversal and the widespread social affliction in Africa. Economically, the shutting down of many of the productive firms, sometimes whole industries resulted in a reduction of the countries' revenue base. Socially, people who had lost jobs suddenly had no means of earning a living. At the same time, Mealie-meal coupons, that is, subsidies on the staple food were removed and at the same time also, prices of essential commodities increased tremendously due to freeing of prices to the market forces of demand and supply. In time, we all started accepting that in order to eat or do anything we needed money. There was nothing for free anymore like it was during Dr. Kaunda's rule. Today, individuals and families have been cut off from economic activities and income.

In terms of the current political dimensions resulting from SAP, the state and the national economy have been compromised. Since the Sub Saharan African State lost its major sources of revenue, it is unable to exercise full sovereignty. The IMF, WTO, World Bank and the donors from the developed countries therefore influence the decisions. More often than not, officials from the international financial institution are among the first people to visit a new head of state in Sub Sahara Africa once inaugurated. In this case, democracy in Africa is questioned. In the African democratic state, the people do not decide on matters affecting them, especially economic matters. This implies that the control of Sub Saharan Africa is by the IMF, World Bank and WTO through the leadership of the United States. This is what president Ronald Reagan aimed at, to control the economies.

Other effects of SAPs include increase in social misfits like a rise in crime rates, street children and prostitution, which in turn increases the rates of HIV/AIDS infection. All over Africa, SAPs have been dreaded and fought by the common man. This has been done through anti-SAP demonstrations, riots and some African governments have experienced coups because the military could not tolerate the effects, as in the case of Zambia. Blood has been shed, lives lost and the suffering continues.

Chapter Six

Africa, Production and International Trade in the Twenty First Century

Before the 1990s, certain commodities in Zambia were a spectacle. Many of us had no idea how the fruit called an apple, a pear or plum looked or tasted like in reality. Those that had the privilege of going overseas brought these commodities as proof of their travel and we would be amazed. There was an Import Substitution Industrialization Strategy (ISIS) in place that forbade the importation of many products from other countries. Apples were an example of the latter. Our country protected infant industries from foreign competition. But these industries were unable to produce enough to meet the domestic market, let alone the international market. And the quality left much to be desired. This scenario obtaining, I remember that my mother would send my aunty (her younger sister) to go very early in the morning to go and line up for cooking oil, sugar and mealie meal. She would come back later in the afternoon, sometimes successful and sometimes not. Production was simply a problem. Our then revered president had the noble desires of making Zambia self sufficient and generating sufficient production which could not be met under the obtaining system.

In chapter two, I discussed the low productivity culture found in Zambia and Africa in general. In this chapter, I will provide a description of this culture's manifestations and the relationship between this culture of low productivity and Africa's performance within the framework of international trade. The general idea is for us to link this culture found in individuals to the really big problem of poverty and squalor it has resulted in.

Economic Activity

	Gross domestic product		Agricultural productivity Agr. Value added per agricultural worker 2000 dollars		Value added as % of GDP							
					Agriculture	Industry	Services	Household final cons. expenditure % of GDP	General gov't. final cons. expenditure % of GDP	Gross capital formation % of GDP	External balance of goods and services % of GDP	GDP implicit deflator Avg. annual % growth
	$ millions 2004	Avg. annual % growth 2004-4	1989-98	2004-3	2004	2004	2004	2004	2004	2004	2004	2004-4
World	40,887,832	2.5 w	.. w	877 w	.. w	.. w	.. w	62 w	17 w	21 w	0 w	..
Low income	1,252,353	5.4	326	375	23	25	52	69	12	22	-3	
Middle income	6,930,704	4.4	..	698	10	34	56	58	13	27	2	
Lower middle income	3,941,575	5.3	413	567	12	37	51	55	13	31	1	
Upper middle income	2,988,438	2.7	..	2,984	7	30	64	62	14	21	3	
Low & middle income	8,183,030	4.6	434	556	12	33	55	58	13	26	1	
East Asia & Pacific	2,367,508	7.5	..	291	15	41	36	47	12	39	2	
Europe & Central Asia	1,764,000	5.0	..	1,856	8	37	61	68	17	23	-1	
Latin America & Carib.	2,018,715	1.5	2,174	2,837	7	23	70	65	12	20	4	
Middle East & N. Africa	600,256	3.5	..	..	14	39	47	62	12	26	-1	
South Asia	874,785	5.4	344	406	22	26	52	69	10	22	-3	
Sub-Saharan Africa	540,990	3.9	312	326	13	28	58	65	14	19	8	
High income	32,715,777	2.0	..	..	..	..	..	61	18	20	1	

Note: a. Data on general government final consumption expenditure are not available; they are included in household final consumption expenditure. b. Data covers mainland Tanzania only.

Source: World Bank. World Development Report 2006. New York:

The table above is on economic activity according to region. The table shows that Sub Saharan Africa's combined Gross Domestic Product (GDP) was lower than all other regions. Yet it has a high population of approximately 400 million. The simple explanation is that Sub-Saharan Africa has the lowest productivity. The table demonstrates this as it shows that in terms of agricultural productivity from 1989 to 1991, the region fell behind all other regions in terms of agriculture value added per agricultural worker. This was the same situation as of 2001 to 2003.

In Africa, there is a saying that what is supposed to be high is low and what is supposed to be low is high. Key indicators of development for Sub Saharan Africa indicate a high population with the highest population growth rate in the world. But the irony comes in as we look at Gross National Incomes and find that Sub Saharan Africa has the lowest GNI in the world. Again the simple economics behind this scenario is low productivity, which yields low exports and therefore low income.

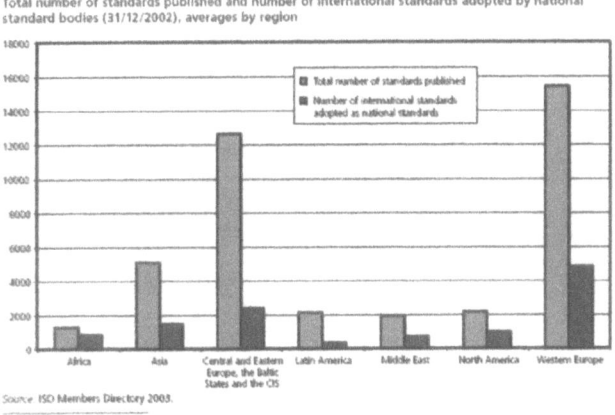

Total number of standards published and number of international standards adopted by national standard bodies (31/12/2002), averages by region

Source: ISO Members Directory 2003.

⁴⁷ See Blind (2004).

⁴⁸ See the case studies in ITC and Commonwealth Secretariat (2003 and 2004).

⁴⁹ See ITC and Commonwealth Secretariat (2004).

Source: World Trade Report 2005. Geneva: World Trade Organisation

In addition to low productivity, Sub Saharan Africa produces low quality or low standard products, both goods and services that are not able to compete favourably on the international market. Such sales are therefore low and contribute to low GNI. The table above shows the total number of standards for goods and services published and the number of international standards for goods and services adopted by national standard bodies as of December 31, 2002 by region. Africa has the lowest number of standards published and the second lowest number of international standards adopted as national standards.

The scenario described in the charts above is the challenge for all of us living in Sub Saharan Africa in the twenty-first century. This is because these charts describe our self-inflicted dismal performance in the most important pillars of the age of globalisation, production.

International Trade and Africa in the 21ˢᵗ Century
The system of international trade is run under international agreements that date back to the years following the great depression. The General Agreement on Tariffs and Trade (GATT) was established in 1944 at Bretton Woods. In 1994, GATT transformed into the World Trade Organisation, WTO.

The WTO provides a forum at which trade negotiations occur. It also ensures that the agreements reached during these negotiations are lived up to by all member countries. The Ministers of Commerce and Trade represent their governments' positions regarding all aspects of trade and negotiate on behalf of their governments vis-à-vis international trade. The trade negotiations are carried out in rounds named after the place where agreements where negotiated and made. The most recent was the Uruguay Round of Trade Negotiations.

Sub Saharan Africa's performance in international trade is a reflection of its low quality and low quantity non-surplus based production of goods and services. This is the major reason why Sub Saharan Africa has had the lowest rate of economic growth and a major reason why it is losing out on the economic benefits of economic globalisation to a country. The basic premise of the World Trade Report 2004[35] was that returns from sound trade and investment policies are dependent on the underlying environment in a range of related policy areas. The WTO argued that policies affecting macroeconomic conditions, infrastructure and infrastructural services, the functioning of domestic markets and the robustness of institutions are key determinants of the ability of countries to benefit from engagement in the international economy. As true as this premise may be for developed countries, I am convinced that returns from sound trade and investment policies in Africa are still simply, basically and specifically dependent on production of surplus high quality production. Let me shed light on the scenario obtaining pertaining to Africa's performance in international trade.

The World Trade Report 2004 reports that as of 2004, 97.5 per cent of international trade took place without Africa's participation[36]. This is a slight improvement from the 1990s when 98 per cent of world trade was taking place without Africa. It further shows that Africa's value of World merchandise trade exports in 2004 was the lowest with trade worth US $228 billion out of US $8.88 trillion worth of world merchandise trade. This further emphasises the low productivity in Africa.

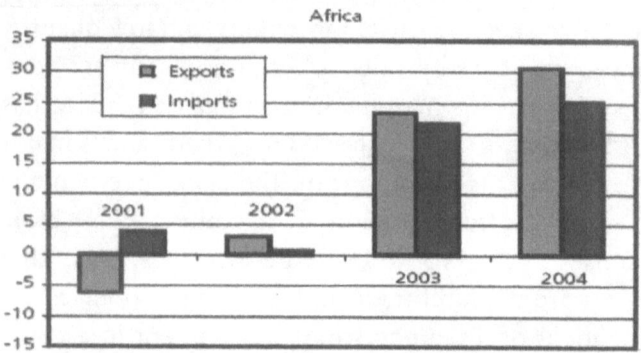

Source: World Trade Report 2005. Geneva: WTO

Africa's exports before 2001, as shown in the chart above, were below zero or in the negatives. With AGOA and the deliberate policies by major industrialised countries to increase imports, Africa has been able to increase exports and its share in international trade.

Sub Saharan Africa's Challenges in International Trade

Despite the near certainty of globalization, Africa is slowly being drifted to the very satellite position and away from the centre of international trade. Africa is facing huge challenges when it comes to participating in international trade for the following reasons, all involving the developed countries and the WTO.

Following the acquisition of independence from colonial powers, Africa slowly drifted away from international political and economic affairs. Not that they are unwilling and unable to participate actively in the international community, but because the developed countries were unwilling to accept African proposals to change the world trade system as it obtained in colonial times. The world trade system has principally remained indifferent from colonial times regarding Africa. Remember that African countries were not in the original plan of the Bretton Woods Institutions, but as sources of raw materials, markets etcetera.

The developed countries have not broken down tariff and non-tariff barriers against African products and FDI. This means that Africa is hardly able to effectively export even the low quantity and quality products to markets of developed countries.

The developed countries continue not to adhere to the WTO rules, regulations and agreements reached during the rounds of trade negotiations. Because of the conditions for aid giving and the conviction and belief that a free world trade system will accelerate social and economic development African countries have adhered to the agreements of the WTO rounds to the dot. The developed countries that advocate for free trade do not adhere in clear stunts of trickery.

In the agricultural sector, developed countries have continued to give their farmers subsidies and to mount taxes against agricultural commodities coming from outside. In 2002 alone, the OECD countries gave a total of US $360 billion to their cotton farmers[37]. "The practice of paying such subsidies to farmers in industrial nations has in recent times faced intense opposition from the developing countries which charge that subsidies foster unfair trade and flood world markets with cheap goods, thereby eroding commodity prices."[38] As a result, African farmers cannot compete with the lower prices and are therefore marginalised from trade. The aid agency, Oxfam argues that production and export subsidies in the developed countries have devastated not only small communities in Africa but entire regions[39]. The the countries in the World Trade Organization are well aware of the lack of commitment to the agreements governing world trade by the developed countries, yet the measures to pressure the breaching and violating governments continue to fail. However, if the violating government is a developing country, the pressure is enormous.

Regional trading blocks have been quite a nuisance excluding imports from Africa. Though the EU has provided for the ACP countries to export certain commodities to European markets, it restricts trade by giving trade quotas and primarily restricting trade within and among its member countries. Meanwhile, African countries have opened up their markets as per WTO rules. Though the creation of regional trading blocks have hindered FDI and African access to markets, the trading blocks in the developed countries have been less affected because it is more a matter of priority for them. Developed countries prioritize trade among themselves than with other regions. For example, it makes economic sense for the United States to trade with Europe and Japan first then other regions and Africa because of the large market. The consequence is that statistic that says 97.5 per cent of world trade takes place without Sub Saharan Africa.

Africa is being marginalized on the basis of the standards I discussed above. May I add that this is largely our own making besides the intellectual property impediment to access machinery that improve quality in our products. The developed countries set standards and regulations for goods and services Sub Saharan countries must meet in order to sale on their market and the international market. For example, commodities must undergo four, five or even six years to be approved for sale on the European Union market. So much as we appreciate high standards, market does exist for lower standard commodities. When I visited the United States in late 2001, I found that in Manhattan, one end of the city sold high quality high price goods worth a fortune. On the other were the kind one would find on an African flea market selling for prices lower than one would find in Sub Sahran Africa. This demonstrates that the market is responsive to people's needs if we let it do its own work without interfering by imposing standards for exports. Imposition of standards on products coming from any country is a protectionist tendency that interferes with trade liberalisation and the free market.

In addition, if at all African producers have to choose to adhere to the standards and regulations, their costs of production would rise. The price of the product will in turn rise and will be unable to compete with the local products of the EU. Therefore, let Africa sell its goods and services the way they are now, the market will deal with matters of standards in due course because it has a way of spontaneously doing it.

Consequences of Low Productivity and Low participation in International Trade

The results of our laxity in production and hardly any significant participation in international trade have brought about an alarming scenario. We will use a measure that the United Nations has developed called the Human Development Index[40]. "The human development index (HDI) is a composite indicator. It covers three dimensions of human welfare: income, education and health. Its purpose is not to give a complete picture of human development but to provide a measure that goes beyond income. The HDI is an instrument for measuring changes in human well-being and for comparing progress in different regions."

From 1995 to 2005, the HDI has been rising across all developing regions, though at variable rates and with the obvious exception of Sub-Saharan Africa. Amid the overall progress, however, many countries suffered unprecedented reversals. Eighteen countries with a combined population of 460 million people registered lower scores on the HDI in 2003 than in 1990. (Only six countries suffered such reversals in the 1980s.) The reversals have been heavily concentrated in two regions. Twelve of the countries are in Sub-Saharan Africa. Just over one-third of Sub-Saharan Africa's population—240 million people—live in countries that have suffered an HDI reversal[41]. Zambia features prominently.

In Sub-Saharan Africa the fatal interaction of economic stagnation or negligible production, slow progress in education and the spread of HIV/AIDS have produced a free fall in HDI ranking. Southern Africa accounts for some of the steepest declines. Thirteen countries out of the eighteen in the world whose HDI ranking has fallen are from this part of the world—a fall of 35 places for South Africa, 23 places for Zimbabwe and 21 places for Botswana[42].

Currently, Sub Saharan Africa has by far the highest number of people living on less than US $1.00 purchasing power parity per day, about 40 per cent[43]. As a matter of definition, when someone is living on less than a dollar per day, they are in extreme or absolute poverty. Chances of survival under these circumstances are minimal. This is the scenario for Zambia vis-à-vis globalisation times which had 86 per cent of its popuplation under the poverty line by the turn of the century.

The war against poverty has witnessed massive reversals and stagnation in Sub-Saharan Africa. The worrying trend for the future is that overall progress is slowing. Much of the success in pushing back poverty over the past two decades was achieved in the 1980s and the first half of the 1990s. Since the mid-1990s $1 a day poverty has been falling at one fifth the 1980–96 rate. This is despite the fact that average growth for developing countries picked up in the 1990s, increasing at more than double the per capita rate of the previous decade. No country has successfully sustained progress in reducing income poverty with a stagnating economy. Average incomes in Sub-Saharan Africa are lower today than in 1990. Recent years have witnessed signs of recovery in several countries, including Burkina Faso, Ethiopia, Ghana, Mozambique and Tanzania. However, recovery has to be put in context. It will take Sub-Saharan Africa until 2012 just to restore average incomes to their 1980 levels at the 1.2% per capita annual growth experienced since 2000.[44]

It is indeed a dismal picture for Africa. At the end of this chapter, the one question that runs through my mind is 'will we survive the age of globalisation?' Think about your own survival, think about what you can do about it.

Chapter Seven

Case Study of Zambia

Low productivity in Zambia

A discourse on Zambia's economic history does not go without boasting that the Zambian economy was once economically stronger than that of the United Kingdom and the United States of America. The point of emphasis is that the Zambian currency, the Kwacha (currency is an indicator of economic strength) was trading one to one with the British pound and that ZMK 1.00 was stronger than US $1.00. It was the high times, and the country was still in excitement immediately after independence.

Zambia achieved independence from almost a century of British colonial rule on October 24, 1964. Our government was led by President Kenneth David Kaunda. Immediately after taking over the country, he maintained the free market economy inherited from the British during the transition to self-determination. Production and exports were high, though it was mainly in raw materials of such mineral resources as copper, lead, zinc and cobalt. In 1964, copper provided ninety-five per cent of total export earnings[45]. Within the first post-independence decade, it was realized that the MNCs from Britain and the United States externalized huge profits leaving the Zambian economy with fewer resources for the pursuit of development programs.

In 1973, nationalization policies were implemented in what the president called Zambianisation of enterprises. The government acquired 51 to 100 per cent of the shares of private enterprises. New state enterprises in the manufacturing, transport, communication and energy sectors were created. The economy was still growing at 10 per cent every year. It was among the most promising economies in Africa and the developing world.

However, world oil price increases and commodity price decreases that shook the global economy in the 1970s gradually affected the Zambian economy negatively. Like many nations, it turned to official development assistance. The debt stock began to steadily increase as a result.

After the IMF and World Bank began to put pressure on developing countries to implement SAP, Zambia was caught up in the pressure in 1985. The government was advised to implement SAP if it were to borrow from the IMF. President Kaunda was reluctant. Further pressure led him to give in, in 1986. Prices were liberalized and they immediately surged causing widespread riots and bloodshed. The president reversed the decision for the next five years. The economy of the country was still competitive.

In 1991, the successor, Frederick J. T. Chiluba accepted the IMF calls. The government embarked on a hasty implementation of SAP famously known as 'Shock

Treatment'. Parastatal companies were sold off to Foreign Direct Investors.

Origins of Culture of Low Productivity

Zambians had always been hard working people until the years that followed independence when the government began to give basic necessities for free to its people. There was free mealie meal using the coupon system, free education including pens, pencils and books, free biscuits, free train and bus rides for young people and so fourth. This is in addition to free accommodation for employees, free electricity, free water and free health services for all.

These free provisions became entrenched on the minds and way of life of the citizens over a period of twenty-seven years when President Kaunda was in power. Over this long period, Zambians lost their value for work and a whole different work ethic ensued. There was no clear connection between work and earning a living. As far as our people were concerned, it was the government's responsibility to take care of each of our needs without our paying for them.

When the Structural Adjustment Programmes set in, every single thing one could think of had to be paid for. Our people were still in inertia until they began to die for lack of basic necessities in the 90s. The drastic transformation in accessing basic necessities was from free to too expensive. There were no jobs, also suddenly.

This culture has continued to this day. It was in the late nineties that some of our people began to value private property and the ethic of working hard in order to earn a living. For many, it was too late to change and so they could not survive. For others, the low productivity culture continues mostly in the public sector as a result of the continuous belief in everything for free. And for the growing generation, adaptation is setting in.

Production Structure of Zambia

The economy has a dual production structure. A highly sophisticated technological sector exists side by side with a large subsistence sector. Currently, the technological sector is concentrated in urban areas from the Copperbelt with copper mining still accounting for over 80 per cent of national income, to Solwezi with more copper mining and to Lusaka with a concentration of manufacturing and services sector. Though the rural sector population-where subsistence production is concentrated- is higher than that of the urban sector, Zambia is a highly urbanized country. The rural sector is characterised by low output and productivity and poor standards of living[46].

Mwanakatwe observed that in the 1990s, there was "a masked disparity in growth rates between the two sectors with all growth and development concentrated in the monetised, mainly urban sector of the economy. Almost without exception... the rural subsistence sector has stagnated." Mwanakatwe attributes this stagnation to the suppression of agriculture producer prices by the government that is keeping food prices down. This is true as it was a direct attack on high productivity in the agricultural sector. The low prices were discouraging higher levels of production and this affected national output.

Mwanakatwe further observes that for the urban sector, the decline in mineral revenue due to the drastic fall in prices at the London Metal Exchange forced the country to go into deficit financing. Efforts made in subsequent years to control increases in recurrent expenditures did not arrest deterioration in deficit financing. Because of these circumstances, there was a lower level of domestic production.

Consequently, there was a serious macro-economic crisis. The inflation rate soared and prices went wild. The interest rates were introduced following SAP and were in unimaginable figures. It was the end of the planned economy and the return of the capitalist economy right at the beginning of the 1990s.

The production structure underwent an overhaul. The following firms were either liquidated or shut down in the first three years. Some of them employed over 3000 people. The Zambia Consolidated Copper Mines had over 50,000 employees.

1. Zambia Airways Corporation (Liquidated National Airline).
2. United Bus Company of Zambia (Liquidated National Road Transport Company).
3. Zambia Consolidated Copper Mines (National Mining Company).
4. Meridian BIAO (Liquidated Pan African Bank).
5. ZCBC (Liquidated Consumer Goods Company).
6. National Import and Export Company (NIECO).
7. FIAT Assembly Plant-Zambia.
8. Luangwa Industries (Bicycle Manufacturing Plant).
9. Kapiri Glass Manufacturing Company (National Glass Factory).

10. Zambia Cooperative Federation (ZCF) (Farmers Cooperative).
11. National Agriculture Marketing Board (NAMBOARD).
12. Zambia Dairy Produce Board (DPB) (National Dairy).
13. ROP Industries (Domestic Oil Producing Company).
14. Prudence Bank
15. Union Bank

The above firms were key to Zambia's economic productivity.

Individual Productivity

Today, Zambian women who worked in senior positions of the above-mentioned enterprises sale vegetables and other groceries at the community markets. Men that were managers and supervisors have occupied the streets, squalid squatters and others are in destitution. Some former workers find some piecework such as carrying someone's shopping or luggage on a wheelbarrow or on their shoulders to the customer's house. In 2003, such work paid ZMK1, 000 to ZMK2, 000 (about US $0.20 to $0.40 cents) depending on the distance. Other former employees have opened taverns. In any squatter compound, one is likely to meet a tavern every five hundred meters.

To adapt to the situation, most people have tried to venture into informal employment. In N'gombe, a squatter township in Lusaka for example, women crush stones to sell to those building houses and men use more of their vocational skills such as carpentry, mechanics (home garages), making roofing sheets and door frames from their domestic premises. Their products are sold to the local community because they cannot compete with those of the MNCs in the city centres. As a matter of fact, N'gombe community has created its own local sub-economy. Goods and services are sold at prices commensurate with the local community's low-income levels.

Other business initiatives being taken are the making of mats and artefacts, specifically targeting the tourist market. I observed this in M'tendere, Northmead in Lusaka and Livingstone in Southern Province. However, the initiatives do not guarantee a regular income and are often characterized by a once in a while sell, especially when it is summer in the developed countries.

However, the saddest part is that the vast majority of Zambians have taken up drinking with the aim of getting drunk with local brews of beer. Men do not even think of grabbing a hoe to go and start a small garden. At an individual level, our youth are not thinking of any new ideas of producing in their natural gifts. There is a loss of will to live and a loss of purpose. The culture of free things has continued to dominate the minds and made sluggards of our youth.

Social Consequences of Lack of Productivity in Zambia
In 1990, 51 per cent of Zambians were living in poverty. After the implementation of SAP, the poverty levels increased by over 30 per cent according to the World Bank. The Central Statistics Office of Zambia disputes this statistic and claims that poverty is at 67 per cent. Whatever the case, it is a high figure. I believe the Bank's statistics are more reliable because their figure has been

confirmed by other studies. In addition, several studies under the UN have also confirmed the same. There has also been a dispute of figures. The CSO claims that Zambia's life expectancy is 52 years. However, a more realistic figure from the World Bank, UN and NGOs is 32 years and that is what we are seeing on the ground.

From World Bank statistics, it can be observed that today, the poorest nation in the world's poorest region of Sub Saharan Africa is Zambia. The chart in the previous chapter also indicates that one's chances of survival in Zambia are the lowest in the world. Eighty six per cent of the 11 million people are impoverished. Put another way, almost 9 million people are living with inadequate or lack of access to the necessities of life in Zambia alone. The 2005 MDG report for Zambia states that 54 per cent of Zambian households can only afford two meals or less per day while 13 per cent can only afford one meal or less per day.

The harsh realities of poverty in Zambia are evident in the stature of the citizens. One will acknowledge that their slim postures are not as a result of a nationwide program of periodic fasting, hunger strikes or slimming diets. The faces tell a story of sorrow though few will want to admit in order to hold on to the little dignity that remains from the better old days. When one asks the urban impoverished the conventional greeting question, 'how are you?' the answer tells much more than its single word; 'surviving'. At a glance, it reveals the struggle for food, jobs, water and homes everyday, carried out in as much a civilized way as one can possibly hold on to.

In June 2002, the president of Zambia Levy Mwanawasa declared a food crisis situation in the country. It is a declaration that was long overdue because the food crisis situation had heightened in 1997 when the results of SAP had reached their peak following a reduction in government spending on agriculture. At that point, villagers and other urban dwellers were, in the local newspapers, reported to go to health centres pretending to be sick in order to have a meal. Others became professional mourners, going for funerals in order to have their meals there. In Africa, no one requires an invitation in order to attend a funeral. People cry, eat and sleep together at the funderal house.

The diet of those living in absolute poverty in Zambia is mainly composed of heavy and stomach filling carbohydrate foods and vegetables. Protein foods apart from the legumes are too expensive for them and are considered a luxury. The maize staple is powdered and cooked into a thick porridge known as 'ubwali' or 'inshima' in the local languages. All in a family eat together at the same time because the quantity is normally too small to leave for anyone who is away.

In a day, the average number of meals ranges from zero to two. Only 33 per cent of households are able to afford three or more meals in a day. Breakfast is normally overridden with lunch being eaten at 2 or 3 o'clock in the afternoon. It may also be considered supper if no miracle of a meal occurs for the evening.

In the densely populated squatter compounds of the capital city, Lusaka, food is sold in small quantities, large enough only to cook one meal. In Garden, M'tendere,

N'gombe and Kalingalinga, all compounds found in Lusaka, I carried out a survey in 2003 and found the reality of the US $1.08 purchasing power parity per day in the expenditure of most households.

US $1.00 = ZM K 5000.00 in 2003 dollars and Kwacha

In M'tendere compound, it is not rare to find a vendor selling a maize cob broken into three equal pieces in order to help the people in the community be able to afford to pay for at least part of the cob. In Chiwempala Township of Chingola in the Copperbelt Province, the city that hosted the giant mining conglomerate, Anglo-American Corporation, most people are unemployed and unable to effectively meet their food requirements. One day I found a family of seven- grandmother, mother, daughter with her two children below age three and two juvenile dependants sitting on a mat outside their house about to finish a meal. The inshima appeared to have been cooked two days before and eaten in parts to ensure a meal everyday for two days. Eaten along with the inshima was kapenta (dried sardines) cooked with out cooking oil, tomatoes or onions. The smallest child, approximately one year old, slowly lifted up the plate to eat the small crumbs left on the metal plates as the mother sorrowfully looks on, probably wishing she could do better for her hungry child.

In the same location, I found another family consisting of grandparents taking care of seven orphans. Grandma makes door rugs for sale in order to feed the family. Grandpa tries to do some carpentry but his eyes and feet were slowly and painfully failing him. The social welfare office was too under funded to help. When I asked about the parents of the children, grandma said they were all her children who had all died.

In Kampumbu, a rural area in the Luangwa Valley near Isoka District, I met a senior citizen, walking slowly for twelve kilometres from his village. On his way, he crossed a dangerous knee deep stream that flows into the Luangwa River. His ailment was the deadly malaria. I did not know what happened to him. It was most likely that he was just given a prescription and no medicine at all, as is the custom nowadays in government clinics and hospitals.

Another incident occurred when I was still a student at the University of Zambia. Across the main road and a few paces from the Main Campus, a man slept besides the road. The story he told me was that he was admitted to Lusaka's University Teaching Hospital; Zambia's main and biggest hospital. He was apparently slightly better, strong enough to go to the toilet so the doctor released him in order to leave his bed space for other apparently more seriously ill patients. But he was still seriously sick and without transport money to get home, 13 km away. He had decided to walk. Such a scene attracted a public outcry for doctors to stop releasing patients until they recovered fully because the majority ended up dying at home. However, what can the doctor do when the hospital is so full that some patients have to share beds while others sleep on mattresses on the floor?

When I was young, I travelled a lot to London and to New York in 2001, I only saw one funeral in New York in a church along Lexington Avenue. A celebrity had lost her life in a plane crush on her way from Mexico. In my short walks in Lusaka alone, I see two or more funerals per day. At the local main cemetery in Lusaka, over twenty burials take place daily. People have been dying without dignity. Most deaths in Zambia are nutrition deficiency and sanitation related in addition to malaria. They can be cured, let alone prevented, but public health and medical services are inadequate. If only the government still produced enough and therefore had the money to support the health and the agriculture sectors, which are the two sectors most affected by SAP.

The poverty description in the preceding chapters is only the tip of the iceberg. One will only be able to know exactly what the African impoverished man, woman and child is going through upon an experience.

Zambia, being the worst affected nation in Sub Saharan Africa has been used to describe the suffering of all other people living in poverty in Sub Saharan Africa as a result of low productivity. Poverty is the same everywhere. It is the lack or inadequate access to the basic necessities of life. It has resulted in the loss of human dignity and respect and caused misery and sorrow for the Sub Saharan Africans. Two thirds of Africans are living under such conditions and 1.6 billion people on our planet experience the above conditions everyday[47]. It can therefore be agreed that there is something wrong with the domestic production system and also as we have seen from the previous chapter, the international economic and political system.

Chapter Eight

Cultural Change

When we ask the right questions, I believe that there is a solution for every problem. And after asking the questions I did, I believe there is still hope for my country and for Sub Saharan Africa. I believe that Sub Saharan Africa is not beyond redemption. Definitely my answers so far are that the state of affairs is seriously dismal, even as the world watches on in a time of world history that surpasses all other times in technological advancement, production and economic progress. My suggestions for Zambia's and Africa's survival in the twenty first century are two-fold; cultural change on the one hand and international cooperation on the other.

Our societies need a transformation of the social fabric beginning at the individual level and ending at the international level. They need a change of culture to adapt to that of the twenty-first century to be in-sync with globalisation. My suggestion begins and ends with this statement; we must individually take personal responsibility for personal change in attitudes and embrace scientific and objective principles, improve productivity, use our power of innovation, love God and man and explore opportunities worldwide. First as individuals, then as a nation and then as a continent. It simply means taking matters into our own hands. You and I must discover our personal interests, our nations' interests and then Sub Saharan Africa's interests and work towards them on the local community, national and international arena.

Each individual African must take an individual development approach to setting he or herself free from poverty. At the same time, he or she must love God and help his or her brother to overcome poverty. Globalization requires and demands an individual contribution and at the same time inter-dependence.

For this to occur we require a voluntary but government led effort toward cultural change. If possible, let everyone undergo a voluntary cultural change course for six months in institutions of learning. A deliberate education policy must be put in place to carry out this process. The contents must address the issues below.

Presidentialism

As individuals, we must respect the presidency but stop acknowledging the omnipotence of the president in Sub Saharan Africa and develop a democratic perspective. A president is not a superhuman being but just an individual we entrust to safeguard our security, our rights and wants.

The presidency must be shaped according to the people's expectations according to democratic principles of government of the people, for the people and by the people as well as accountability. There must be a clear distinction between the public and private domains of the man holding the office of president. We must be able to shape the boundaries of his or her power. This will involve legislative action as well as interest articulation through petitions and or public demonstrations.

In Zambia, it has often been said that the president possesses too much power. One of the debates came up in 2006 over whether the National Assembly or the president should set the date of elections due to take place later that year. The president unexpectedly announced the date and tried to justify his decision through some propaganda. The nation accepted and forgot. People have a democratic right to have an input into how their nation is being run, hence checking the power of the president is democratically and politically correct.

More importantly, the National Assembly and other public institutions must be able to advise the president whenever he goes beyond his/her presidential domain.

An important point is that we must begin advocating for the use of a merit system in all circles. All public servants must be employed on merit. Personal favours using public office must be prosecuted.

Though I have stated the above, the system of presidentialism is a rigid one because history has shown that presidents are unwilling to relinquish powers institutionally and or constitutionally. Nonetheless, the president is best placed to initialize an aggressive policy of voluntary cultural change.

Ethnicism and Clientelism

As individuals, we must begin to look at each other beyond ethnic identities and begin to appreciate each person as an individual, recognising the value that each individual's personality can bring to the life of our nation and continent and the world at large. The greatest commandment is first to love God with one's soul, heart, and might and secondly, to love others as self.

Respect for God and respect and tolerance for all individuals, other ethnic groups and respect for the rule of law is the antidote to the negative consequences of the ills of ethnicism and clientelism. Africans must exhibit a true spirit of brotherhood. The Lord Jesus Christ and other notable religious figures and religions emphasize the brotherhood of mankind for peaceful co-existence and societal progress. In this regard, an African individual must have imbedded in his sub-conscious to 'do unto my brother as my brother would do unto me for our prosperity.' Individuals must learn to mind and respect the brother nearby or next door. Whatever would hurt a fellow African, a fellow human being must be avoided to its minute detail.

Among the most difficult challenges to be overcome in all of Africa is the virtue of integrity and honesty. Each individual must learn the importance of doing what he says and saying what he does. The lack of integrity inevitably leads to the absence of trust, such as that prevailing among Africans today. Therefore, each individual must cultivate in him the virtue of integrity and beyond that, trust. The point at which each individual African will have integrity and then trust for his brother will be the apex of the African identity and the establishment of the road to overcoming poverty in the twenty first century. It can be done, there is a lot we can learn from other parts of the world, in this case the Scandinavian countries have done it, and they are human beings just like all Africans.

The Sub Saharan African governments portray a picture of pursuing a vigorous anti-corruption fight because they have to impress donors. Corruption in Sub Saharan Africa is culturally embedded in acts of ethnicism and clientelism and represents a clash between African formal culture and the Weberian Theory of Bureaucracy. Inefficiency has been observed in that no goals have been set regarding the target percentage by which governments aim to reduce corruption as is the case in Zambia. In addition, more funds are being utilized on operation costs of the anti-corruption agencies than is being recovered. I believe corruption will be well dealt with under the process of cultural change and economic empowerment.

Low Productivity and Lack of Culture of Surplus Productivity

In all that we do, as Sub Saharan Africans, we must invest massively our time and effort to produce our goods, services and activities in surplus, beyond what is required. The time when we were receiving all basic necessities for free has gone. As long as globalization is in place- and it is not going away- nothing is for free. There will never be anymore government help in form of subsidies or coupons, that's where we are headed. This time it is individual productivity that reigns. This goes especially to the subsistence farmers. It is of absolute necessity to produce enough even for export to the developed world because we need to generate that revenue for national development and ultimately, survival in the twenty first century.

In the rural economy, there must be intensified training of peasant farmers so that they begin to develop a culture and habit of producing in surplus. Training schemes must be put in place. Agriculture specialists must be sent to all areas of agricultural activity to train the farmers in appropriate modern methods. Latest developments in agro-technology must be discussed at such sessions. Practical sessions on the application of agricultural knowledge must be emphasized. The sessions can be the point of exodus from the unproductive traditional methods. In fact, some traditional methods, such as shifting cultivation, have been cited as a detriment to the environment. The training sessions can be opportunities to inform incentives from the state for farmers' participation in agriculture in the free market system.

In the rural economy, what is most important is to ensure that Africa overcomes the food crisis and achieve food security. The endorsement and implementation of a policy of state responsibility/ownership of at least two-thirds of Africa's agriculture sector will achieve this. The other third can be committed to the private sector.

Due to SAP, the agricultural sectors of Sub Saharan African countries in the past have not supplied enough food for consumption by the local population. Firms have been pressured to produce cash crops for export causing neglect of the domestic market. This is the reason behind Africa's expensive policy of importation of food for consumption.

Therefore, the African states can for example invest in state farms that can produce food for the domestic market albeit run on market principles. The state farms can also be vital for the creation of employment especially that the majority of the African population is directly involved with the agriculture sector. The state can buy the machinery for every state farm, appoint a manager, and train every employee on how to use the equipment. Later, such farms can be floated on the stock market. I suggest this bearing in mind that no economy can completely be a free market based economy. For a while, the state can have its own investments in vital sectors for the good of the nation and agriculture is one sector that will need government intervention.

The solving of problems in the agriculture sector can result in the sorting of many more African problems. This is so because the growth in the agriculture sector will result in the growth in the industrial sector, bearing in mind the theory of balanced growth. A boost in one sector results in a boost for others due to sectoral inter-dependence.

In this way, poverty can greatly be reduced. Expenses on medicine, treatment of patients and the death rate can reduce because of enhanced nutrition. As has been noted, the majority of deaths and health complications in Africa are caused by nutrition deficiency. With enough food, people can be healthy and may not require much of health services. They would channel their energy and mental faculties to the achievement of individual development and ultimately African development.

The idea of state intervention in the agriculture sector or rural economy is an unpopular one with the IMF, World Bank and WTO. Therefore individual farmers must take it upon themselves to produce in surplus with minimal government interventions. However, it is currently a matter of survival for the impoverished in Africa. Besides, though the developed countries do not require intervening in a free market system, they provide subsidies and other forms of intervention for their farmers while fully aware of WTO rules and agreements. Therefore, Africa must pursue the right policies for the present and then pursue IMF, World Bank and WTO policies when the conditions are appropriate, that is, when people stop dying as a result of their policies.

Sub Saharan African industries must in the manufacturing and other sectors establish and increase production in order to survive competition in the global village. Globalisation operates on the principles of comparative and competitive advantages. For Africa, it must maximize production in raw materials and begin processing into finished products. At the same time, processing factories can be established for an improvement in the production of value added commodities. Africa must also find a way to determine its own prices of its raw material exports.

The emergence of Africa out of poverty and into prosperity lies in its ability to produce high standard products in surplus and find markets for its produce. African raw materials are already on demand in the developed countries. But Africa must begin to produce its own manufactured goods for its own market.

I hold the view that one African currency must be introduced and strengthened against major trading currencies such as the US dollar. The stability of a single African currency will depend on Africa's surplus production and increased export in international trade as opposed to imports.

Pertinently, there must be a sustained effort by African leaders to urge Africans to buy African products. This can enable the provision of strong competition of products and services from MNCs. However, African producers and investors must promote the highest standards of quality of their products and services. They must aim at satisfying the global tastes and quality.

Life in the global village demands that at some point, products must be able to appeal to the multicultural, multi-racial, multi-lingual and international social community. Globalization does not only emphasize the globalization of production, but the globalisation of distribution as well. Sub Saharan Africa must embark on a road to producing in surplus, high quality goods and services that meet the tastes of the global village.

It is important that leaders play an important role of boosting African private sector production by considering as a priority, the awarding of contracts to indigenous African local investors. An emphasis here is placed on the construction sector. If Africans are to be a proud people that will maintain their structures, they will have to build their own land. They will have to design and build their own infrastructure. South Africa is already playing a major role by manufacturing capital goods required in construction and other manufacturing processes and supplying them to Sub Saharan African states.

What will be vital is the creation of strong linkages between the urban industrial sector and the rural agriculture sector. Local urban industrial sector can provide the rural agriculture sector with the appropriate technology. The technology must be made as a result of local research on the specifications required by farmers to effectively and efficiently produce in African conditions. African agriculture technological requirements are unique to it. Intermediate technology is what is needed because it takes into consideration labour intensity in Africa. Put another way, the industrial sector can supply farming implements such as tractors, fertilizers, hybrid seeds, ploughs and hoes. The agriculture sector in turn can supply the raw materials and food requirements of the people working in the industrial sector.

To develop the strong linkages, our transport infrastructure to rural and world market centres must be developed upon. Globalization necessitates the interconnectedness of each individual, physically or electronically, for mutual benefit in the global village. This means that each individual African farmer must be accorded the opportunity to offer his commodities and services to the global market and also to benefit from cheaper sources of commodities from the wider world through transport infrastructure. There must be a physical link to rural farmers. The African states can implement this by building more roads and railway lines to remote areas. This will enable farmers to travel and transport their agricultural produce to market centres. Without such action, the states will be denying a significant percentage of Africans from being given the opportunity to enjoy the benefits of global citizenship and the means to making a living.

Sub Saharan Africa will only be able to stand on its own if it takes an individual approach to the continent's development of a culture of surplus productivity. Each individual African leader and citizen must take an interest in setting production goals and knowing the general level of productivity. Each must learn Sub Saharan Africa's potentials and the opportunities available to him to produce, play a role in international trade and develop the continent.

The basic argument here is simply that Sub Saharan Africa must increase productivity to higher quality surplus levels in the international economy in relation to the IMF, World Bank and WTO. Sub Saharan African leaders can impart the culture of surplus productivity by enshrining the school curriculum with the rationale behind surplus productivity, which in actual fact is international trade. Globalisation requires accurate knowledge and understanding of global productivity and international trade.

If we teach our children this culture when young, we may be giving them a better chance to survive globalization and live long fruitful and productive lives far much better than we could have dreamt. I see a day when Sub Saharan Africans will be at the top of global output and key stakeholders on the world market. I see Sub Saharan

Africa and Zambia in particular influencing global economic trends and playing a major role in international trade negotiations. All we have to do is change our culture for the better.

Chapter Nine

Economic Cooperation with the IMF, World Bank and WTO

The right way for Africa vis-à-vis the *Washington Consensus* policies will be to more comprehensively adopt the economic policies because ignoring them will exacerbate the marginalization of the continent and its people from global production and international trade. Unfortunately or fortunately, there is overwhelming evidence in the fall of the Soviet Union that the policies suggested in the *Washington Consensus* are the most efficient for economic growth.

However, a slower, more cautious approach to economic and social consequences must be used through the integration of social safety nets during implementation regardless of how much pressure comes from the IMF, World Bank and WTO. Though already too late to deal with the so-called "Shock-Treatment" that was used during the twentieth century, I believe we learned our lessons. "Shock treatment" was not good for Sub Saharan Africa especially for the social distribution of resources, as it produced huge figures of social casualties. In this regard, Sub Saharan African governments must continue implementing the Washington Consensus policies with more social and economic caution. My point is that it is not too late to shape these policies in a more Sub Saharan Africa friendly manner.

Once the policies in chapter eight are in place, Sub Saharan African countries should adopt more comprehensively the trade liberalization policy in order to be able to effectively sustain its presence in international trade, albeit after a cost benefit analysis. But again on two conditions; that the IMF, World Bank and WTO ensure that developed countries open their markets to goods coming from Sub Saharan Africa; and that our leaders are put to task to represent us by doing a good job at pressuring the developed countries to breakdown all tariff and non-tariff barriers to trade. That is their job and we must respectfully speak out, negotiate and see to it that they work, not fear them.

The continent is taking a big economic risk by opening the market while those of developed countries remain highly protected. The result will reflect in the worsening of the already catastrophic balance of trade deficits, the very situation the IMF aims to correct. Globalization must be directed towards fair global economic trading rules. Hence, all countries must have equal access to the global market under a liberal trading system. As pointed out, under the Lome Agreement of the African, Caribbean and Pacific group of states and European Union (ACP-EU) trading group, the ACP countries are allowed to export a fixed amount of sugar to the European Union market under a quota allocation[48]. It must also be added that by 1997, under this agreement the EU was only importing 3.4 per cent of its total imports from ACP countries. This represents unfair terms of trade because the EU can do better than that.

Trade liberalization if followed strictly by all countries would allow African countries to freely export and freely import goods and services, which would create a locally and internationally competitive economy. On the other hand, countries in the European Union can export manufactured goods to Africa without restriction. African governments however must learn to place reservations or bans on the importation of certain goods. This is in reaction to agriculture subsidies being given to farmers in Europe, North America and Japan by their governments in order to cut down on losses. Subsidies ensure that goods from these countries are sold cheaper on the international market, therefore generating unequal competition on the part of Africa. By the time the Cancun, Mexico talks of WTO collapsed in 2002, Africa had lost about US $310 billion in 2002 alone[49]. The cause was that African cash crops could not find market in the presence of the cheaper crops from the developed countries.

Africa should adopt the policy of privatization more comprehensively based on a policy deliberately aimed at transferring ownership of public enterprises and pubic businesses and in very lucrative cases private ones to local and domestic investors. This will help boost productivity. The IMF and World Bank have pressured the governments to privatize economically productive sectors, often the economic backbones of the country. The continued privatisation of public enterprises in which foreign investors are the sole or major shareholders have left Sub Saharan African countries with a reduced revenue base. Though these companies pay tax, foreign investors are allowed to repatriate up to 70% of their profits from Zambia and other Sub Saharan African countries in what is commonly known as capital flight. This means that if the situation subsists, African development in real terms will halt or may reverse for much of the development funds will be repatriated. On the contrary, if local and domestic private investors acquire shares in these companies, the profits will remain in the country and will be re-invested. Therefore, African leaders must develop policies and mechanisms that will empower local entrepreneurs through majority ownership of local enterprises.

I am aware of the question raised by many to say few Africans have the financial capital to invest, how can they acquire these companies as private investors? The answer lies in the extension of the current investment incentives offered to foreign investors to local private investors. Governments must provide local entrepreneurs with loans, on concessionary terms- less emphasis on collateral- for investment and allow them to buy over 50% of shares of each of the companies short listed for privatization. It will economically empower Sub Saharan Africans in the twenty first century economic dispensation through access to an income and reduce unemployment and the impact that privatization- which has come along with cutting down a company's workforce- has had of cutting Africans from earning a decent living in the past decade to this day. In fact in the current scenario, this is the best way of creating employment and raising the GNI.

It is further important to point out that the uncritical belief in and acceptance of privatization- of course coupled with pressure from the Bretton Woods Institutions- led most African countries to initiate the programme by privatizing their major revenue earning companies and industries. It would have been logical to begin with the sectors less impacting on the economy and to see how the programme would perform.

African governments must learn to harmonize the liberalized interest rates bearing in mind the high inflation rate. They must acknowledge the perpetually high demand on the market for loans from banks and other financial lending institutions. Governments must concentrate on reducing and stabilizing the inflation rates so that the value of money people borrow does not lose value yet at the same time the interest rate increase. In a broader sense, interest rate liberalization represents financial liberalization, which Sub Saharan Africa has implemented to an extent. The implication for Sub Saharan Africa is that it has let the market determine the rate or price at which money is borrowed. In the current situation, there is still some government intervention through the central banks. By determining how much the commercial banks bank with the central banks in Africa, they are able to determine how much money is available for loans. The interest rate then must reflect the market situation.

In essence, by saying a competitive exchange rate in describing the *Washington Consensus*, Williamson meant an economy competitive with other economies because the exchange rate or value of a currency represents the value of the economy as compared to other economies. Most Sub-Saharan African currencies except for the South African Rand and Botswana Pula are far from competitive in the global economy. Whether pegged to the US dollar or the CFA Franc, the currency must reduce to single digit levels, which in economic terms is regarded as competitive. Again, the proposed way is to increase the productivity of all economic activities to high quality surplus levels, finding markets and exporting to generate foreign exchange. Upon improving productivity, Sub Saharan Africa must exhaust all diplomatic efforts to negotiate for fair terms of trade or more specifically, determine and/or sell its goods and services at market determined prices on the international market, not to leaving it to the developed countries to determine the prices. If left without being addressed, this will become a perennial problem for Africa's participation in the global village.

Sub Saharan African countries have put in place among the most attractive Foreign Direct Investment (FDI) incentives and must continue with this. It is the most efficient way of raising capital for the economy through the large Multinational Corporations (MNCs). However, it must be accepted that Sub Saharan Africa has a very small market size, not based on population size but on income size. There are fewer people with an income than the MNCs can sell.

In reciprocity, Sub Saharan Africa must develop its participation in FDI itself. Again this will require increased productivity to high quality surplus levels. In the globalization of production, it is profitable and possible for Sub Saharan Africa to produce goods from other countries at a cheaper production cost than at home. Since 1970, Africa has had over US $ 1 billion of the inward flow of FDI[50]. During the same period, Sub Saharan African countries had trace values of outward flow of FDI. It is vital to add that at the same time, less than a third of FDI was re-invested while the rest was repatriated.

The aim of government in tax reform as a *Washington Consensus* policy is to create a tax system that should reflect a broad tax base and one that does not substantially reduce the net income of its citizens. This can be done by capturing those economic activities not yet captured. It can also be done by capturing those individuals in the informal sector, not captured in the tax system yet earn a reasonably taxable income such as charcoal producers, private taxi and minibus drivers. However, it must be noted that the urban and industrial sectors in Sub Saharan Africa are not large enough for the economy to benefit significantly from the tax system. This means that those in industry have a large tax burden imposed on them unless higher production levels are achieved.

Sub Saharan Africa must by far do better in its efforts of practicing fiscal discipline. It is vital that governments spend only the revenue they generate and remain within the confines of the budget. This as much as possible must be the focus of government economic efforts. It is appalling that Sub Saharan African governments have not learned that the money overspent must still be accounted for. Whether it came in form of loans, grants or technical assistance, the nations pay it back in one form or the other. Though it will be inevitable for Sub Saharan Africa to take up the option of borrowing locally and internationally, careful consideration must be given to the development of a viable plan through which governments will be able to pay back, without jeopardizing the development process, as was done in the past four decades of aid and the consequent debt. It is also encouraging that careful implementation of many of the Washington Consensus policies has attracted financing for development from bilateral relations, multilateral agencies and cooperating partners as noted in those countries that attained the Highly Indebted Poor Country (HIPC) completion point, including Zambia in 2005.

The importance of property rights for the productive operation of an entrepreneurial economy cannot be over-emphasized in Sub Saharan Africa. This should be at an affordable cost. In the currently ongoing democratization and economic liberalization process across the continent, property rights must be given their deserving sanctity as merits any twenty first century capitalist system. This will also be central in the attraction of foreign investment.

The deregulation of administrative controls on goods and services within Sub Saharan Africa's borders must be removed. This does not however mean there should not be any controls especially on waste management. Environmental controls must be placed on toxic production of toxic waste in manufacturing industries.

The government must more comprehensively prioritize expenditure. It must stop interpreting reordering of public expenditure priorities as public expenditure cuts and see it as reordering priorities. The Zambian government has been buying luxury cars at exorbitant prices when people are dying of hunger in rural areas and health centres. Expenditure must be directed towards agriculture, basic health, education, the environment and infrastructure development in addition to surplus production incentives.

By our experience of the 1990s, the Washington Consensus policies tended to socially displace people and consequently threw them into chronic poverty. Privatization of over 260 state owned enterprises and public sector reform resulted in the increase of the unemployment rate to over 80% in Zambia alone[51]. Those negatively affected by the Washington Consensus policies need relief, compensation and redeployment into meaningful economic contribution today. They must first be given relief in that they must be given basic needs such as food and shelter, perhaps through food aid from local reserves, and a small loan in any viable form for a given period until they are able to sustain themselves. It can be a goat, money or a cow or even seeds and fertiliser. Social safety nets in Africa must be public ones instituted in the government structures. This argument is not a contradiction to my stance on individuals engaging in surplus productivity because in this case I am talking about people who are in extreme poverty such that such an intervention or the lack of it means life or death.

Chapter Ten

International Cooperation: the Panacea in the 8th Millennium Development Goal and in Africa's Survival in the Twenty First Century

The backdrop of any panacea to Africa's development problems inevitably involves international cooperation, which is the main thrust of the eighth Millennium Development Goal (8th MDG). The eighth MDG states as follows; "Develop a global partnership for development." My recommendation is that if Sub Saharan African countries are to achieve a one out of eight MDG grade, it must be the 8th MDG. With less than a decade to go, questions of attainment, let alone sustainability of the Mdgs have been raised from all corners of the globe. In this chapter, I suggest that international cooperation under the 8th United Nations MDG provides the foundation as well as the political will for the attainment and sustainability of Sub Saharan Africa's survival in the twenty first century.

The Millennium Development Goals (MDGs) were formulated during the United Nations (UN) Millennium

Summit under the distinguished leadership of former Secretary General Kofi A. Annan. At the summit, a first in the new millennium held in September of 2000 at the UN headquarters in New York, the 191 Heads of State and Government present recognised their collective responsibility. They acknowledged their national and international obligation to uphold the principles of human dignity, equality, and equity. These principles were adopted and documented into the United Nations Millennium Declaration adopted by the Fifty-fifth UN General Assembly on 18 September 2000. The Millennium Declaration was then developed into what are now known as the MDGs. The Heads of State and Government committed their nations to meeting the MDGs by the year 2015.

The 8th MDG simply requires that nations "Develop a global partnership for development."[52] It contains seven targets, that is, (five or six more targets than the other MDGs). This should be the first signal of its pertinence. I will focus on targets 12, 13 and 18 while bearing in mind the rest of the targets. The three targets read as follows;

Target 12: "Develop further an open, rule based, predictable, non-discriminatory trading and financial system (includes a commitment to good governance, development, and poverty reduction- both nationally and internationally)." ;

Target 13: "Address the special needs of the Least Developed Countries (includes tariff –and quota-free access for Least Developed Countries' exports, enhanced program of debt relief for heavily indebted poor countries [HIPCs] and cancellation of official bilateral debt, and more generous official development assistance for countries committed to poverty reduction).

Target 18: "In cooperation with the private sector, make available the benefits of new technologies, especially information and communications technologies."

An analysis of the 8th MDG reveals that its attainment will provide the developing countries with the underlying framework and paradigm for the achievement of economic growth and development through fair trade, access to western markets, increased ODA and debt relief.

The scenario proposed by the community of nations in the 8th MDG is that of which Sub Saharan African and other developing countries can take advantage of by increasing production to surplus levels since a vent would have been provided for surplus production and therefore increased income through export growth.

The 8th MDG is the only one that is supply side (production oriented) while the rest of the seven MDGs are demand side (consumption oriented). We cannot spend on all seven MDGs without earning through the 8th MDG. Developing countries, especially those in Sub Saharan Africa have accepted the notion that it makes sense to consume what you do not produce, that is, bilateral and multilateral budgetary assistance in form of grants, loans and technical assistance. The sense that Sub Saharan African governments have to now embrace is that they can only spend what their nations produce because in retrospective analysis, African countries have still had to pay back huge sums for debt servicing and in form of conditionalities tied to Aid.

The 8th MDG further suggests a level economic and political playing field by establishing a 'global partnership'. Zambia and any other Sub Saharan government needs global partners in its quest to develop. In addition, debt relief and increased ODA will accelerate development programs as resources will be diverted from debt servicing and increase the pool of resources respectively.

Following the collapse of the Soviet Union and the subsequent acceleration of the process of globalization, the world has embraced hope at the renewed commitment to the development of the developing countries and to Sub Saharan Africa in particular. The alarming concern that Sub Saharan Africa has lagged behind all continents in terms of reaping the benefits of globalization has in recent times prompted renewed commitment to the continent. The climax came with the former British Prime Minister's involvement. In a speech to the October 2001 Labour Party conference, Tony Blair foresaw a new global consensus that would deliver an end to poverty in Africa[53]. This was followed up by the establishment of the Blair Commission for Africa in February 2004, with the assistance of rock star Bob Geldof and Chancellor of the Exchequer, now Prime Minister Gordon Brown.

Commitment to Africa's development was further enhanced by the release of the Millennium Project Report to the UN Secretary General led by Columbia University's Professor Jeffery D. Sachs in January 2005. What is interesting is that both the Blair Commission for Africa and Professor Sachs' team recommend a substantial increase in Official Development Assistance (ODA) to Africa. Africa certainly requires ODA in substantial amounts.

They simply agree to giving developing countries the 0.7% of the budgets of developed and industrialised countries that the G8 committed to and renewed to achieve in the Monterrey Consesus.

It is a well known fact that Africa has been receiving ODA for over four decades since the years of attainment of independence. It need not be mentioned that this has not achieved development but merely increased the debt burden and kindled much academic debate about the effectiveness of ODA in the development of Africa. However, this commitment of the international community especially through the precepts of the 8th MDG will add the vital ingredient in the African development recipe if really the G8 bring it to fruition.

To a critical mind, perhaps there is a different picture as we consider the interests, costs and sacrifices as compared to the gains the G8 are bound to make. Targets 12 and 13 of the 8th MDG pose perhaps the greatest challenges to and question the commitment of the rich industrialized countries to genuine development and to international cooperation with poorer states. For these countries, opening their markets, committing to fairer trade and increased ODA in addition to debt relief are where they stand to lose the most. It has been so historically, and so is it now.

The Bible speaks of a parable in which a man diligently knocks on his neighbour's door, even at a late hour, until his neighbour opens for him and he gets what he wants. After over three decades of calls for the precepts of the 8th MDG- which have historically come in different forms and fallen on deaf ears, there is strong reason to believe that the rich and powerful countries are finally cooperating with their lesser counterparts.

Advocacy for fair trade, access to production capital, increased ODA and debt relief were among the propositions raised by the G77 (Group of 77 Third World Countries) in the 1970s to the late 80s under the proposition for a New International Economic Order (NIEO). However, the NIEO was constantly removed off the international development agenda in favour of 'Cold War' politics. Through the eyes of an optimist, there is significant correlation with the parable for poor countries considering the current trends of international commitment to developing countries, especially Sub Saharan Africa, even at this late hour.

Notwithstanding this seemingly convincing argument, Dipak Patel[54], Zambia's former Minister of Commerce Trade and Industry and former WTO Coordinator for the LDC Group of Commerce in 2005, made a critical observation in an article entitled 'The Trinity of Aid, Fair Trade and Debt Relief'. He stated that "the ingenious use of the English language by our developed partners to appease the LDCs is now getting to be too far fetched… There has to be some sense of integrity and credibility with what is agreed… During the Uruguay Round, we agreed that "Members shall take account of special needs of developing countries… [In] The Doha Development Round…part of the mandate reads "the majority of the

WTO members are developing countries. We seek to place their needs and interests at the heart of the work programme adopted in this declaration" and went on to say "all special and differential treatment provisions shall be reviewed with a view to strengthening them and making them more precise, effective and operational." By the time of the Cancun talks, the developing countries observed that none of these agreements were implemented by the developed countries.

Careful examination of the language used clearly mentions "taking account of LDC special needs" and not meeting the special needs. It also mentions "seeking to place" their needs at the heart of the work programme and not placing their needs at the heart of the work programme. The above, in addition to their track record in committing to WTO agreements, questions the commitment of the developed countries to the MDGs and to international cooperation for development.

In terms of language use, for three decades the G77 were seeking a statement whose wording could amount to half an A4 size paper with signatures taking up more paper; something close to this;

'By the next WTO Round, all countries agree to; implementing policies and mechanisms of fair trade, breaking down all trade barriers, and the barriers of access to production capital; all WTO members commit to implement by the next round, 100 per cent cancellation of all bilateral and multilateral debt owed by developing countries; the G8 to provide 0.7% of their income to ODA for developing countries; to develop production infrastructure; and to develop the export sector.'

The details of such an agreement would then remain to be worked out by the technocrats. The above represents part of what the 8th MDG is proposing to achieve by the year 2015.

At the lead of the community of nations is the United States of America. In this regard, Washington's commitment to leading the community of nations in achieving the MDGs, specifically the 8th MDG, is a fair measure of global commitment to attaining the goals. In this vein, in an article in *Foreign Affairs Magazine*, Sachs[55] observed that worldwide, including the country's own politicians and citizens, people believe that the United States leads in global concern towards international development.

"Ironically though, this outpouring of concern may obscure rather than clarify a deeper truth. Other than in response to disasters- famines, floods and earthquakes- US assistance for the world's poorest countries is utterly inadequate. It falls far short of meeting the needs of recipient countries… does not fulfil Washington's many promises to fund development adequately."

In his following remark, Sachs brings to the fore words that Secretary General Ban Ki Moon and the international community must bear in mind for the next decade until 2015; Professor Sachs says

"Without a new approach, Washington risks undermining the most important international development goals that the world has accepted- and plunging the international community into a maelstrom of recrimination."

Considering the interacting factors in the current state of international cooperation, the 8th MDG is achievable on the basis of three important considerations. The first refers to the degree of reconcilability between the interests of the G8 as led by Washington and the group of Sub Saharan and other developing countries. The second refers to the power and influence that each group is able to successfully employ in systematic diplomatic negotiations. The third and of considerable importance refers to the effectiveness of the Office of the UN Secretary General in his role as arbitrator and in whom is vested the responsibility of ensuring global conflict resolution and international cooperation.

These considerations are under the assumption that all parties have substantial faith in and commitment to targets 12 and 13 of the 8th MDG as they have declared. Another assumption is that both the G8 and developing countries value international cooperation with the sanctity that it deserves and with the Secretary General's level of commitment. Sub Saharan African countries must embrace this point religiously.

As I see it, the G8 will have to forgo billions of dollars in tax payers' money by forgiving the debt of not only the HIPCs but may ultimately meet the debt relief needs of all other developed and developing countries in the next 10 years?

Secondly, opening their markets to cheaper goods coming from the developing regions will expose their producers to fierce competition. World trade at the rate of 97.5 per cent taking place without Sub Saharan African countries may mean that Africa may not significantly affect international trade even with this measure in place. However, progressively and in the long term, the cheaper products may in actual fact prove to present significant competition.

Thirdly, the provision of ODA in the form of grants is a further financial and technical loss on the part of G8 countries. The politics of ODA have been brought to the fore for the past half century of development Aid. Professor Jeffrey Sachs in his *The End of Poverty*[56] argues that a one time boost of aid in Sub Saharan countries can help millions that are in extreme poverty climb the first rung of the ladder that leads to escaping their poverty. I believe this is an important option the world must follow. The point here is that it will require a substantial sacrifice by the developed countries, one that requires substantial examination and political will never before seen.

Fourthly, from target 18, making available the benefits of new technology may imply the reform and possible relaxation of intellectual property laws and patent rights.

Against the above losses, it is difficult to fathom the idea that the developed countries only stand to gain international credibility and a thank you from the developing countries. In this regard, it is only logical to conclude that the developed countries will gain more power over developing countries through conditionalities most likely to be imposed, just like debt cancellation has in recent times been coming with its own conditions.

As regards losses for the developing countries, it is likely that full attainment of the eighth MDG will be a challenge especially for the poor Sub Saharan African states in safeguarding their sovereignty due to the conditionalities.

The eighth MDG will continue to provide excellent conditions for the operations and activities of MNCs, precipitating capital flight. In addition, these countries will be exposed to speculative short term portfolio investment, especially that capital markets would have grown due to the increase in FDI flows to developing countries (in addition to investor confidence as a result of debt relief). This form of investment is undesirable for Sub Saharan Africa and any developing country because it has the ability to destabilise entire economies within a very short time.

On the other hand, the gains for Sub Saharan Africa and the rest of the developing world will be all that these countries have always wanted, that is, a step towards economic freedom albeit with conditionalities to meet. But it will be a great leap to the survival of Sub Saharan Africa in the twenty-first century.

In terms of the power and influence that each group has potential to employ in systematic diplomatic negotiations, it is the practice rather than the norm that in the community of nations, in which all nations are considered equal, the G8 possess an upper hand despite being in numerical minority, not forgetting that the United States is the sole superpower that hold the world in balance.

The power and influence of developing countries vis-à-vis diplomatic negotiations lies in their being a numerical majority and not on nuclear power and of course, financial superiority. Therefore they will find strength in multilateral based negotiations and a definite weakness in bilateral based negotiations. Numerical majority has from history's lessons achieved some successes especially when developing countries stuck together at WTO on the cotton subsidies. The biggest battle occurs when the developed countries bring down the negotiations to the bilateral level, at which point Sub Saharan African and other developing countries fail to bite the fingers that feed them. This weakness must be turned into strength by developing capacity among diplomats in the power of negotiation.

As the institution responsible for international cooperation, the Office of the United Nations Secretary General will have to strengthen its role as arbitrator between all nations weak and strong, rich and poor through the sacrosanct paths of international cooperation. In a widely read article, former Secretary General Kofi Annan[57] stated that

"Dealing with today's challenges requires broad, deep and sustained global co-operation. Countries working together can achieve things that are beyond what even the most powerful state can accomplish by itself.

Those who drew up the charter of the United Nations in 1945 saw these realities very clearly. Their purpose was not to usurp the role of the sovereign states but to enable states to serve their people better by working together."

It must therefore be acknowledged that international cooperation is the fulcrum of the achievement of Sub

Saharan Africa's productivity and economic growth, the MDGs and especially the eighth MDG. It is the fulcrum upon which the developing countries must place their practical attention and messianic hopes to eradicate poverty.

International cooperation however has its own weaknesses that must be addressed. The major weakness is that International cooperation is voluntary. The United Nations Secretary General cannot impose it upon any state or government. In this regard, as the member states continue to pursue reform of the world body, equal attention must be given to strengthening the Office of the Secretary General on its responsibilities in presiding over international cooperation.

To measure the eighth MDG's success, the question to ask is 'how and to what extent is international cooperation feasible, especially against a backdrop of conflicting interests between the developed and developing worlds with less than a decade before 2015?

This is pertinent because firstly, the MDGs are a current representation of the many agreements made by the international community deemed for the benefit of the poorer nations, which have been broken time and again. In answering the above question it must be emphasized that without the strong leadership of the UN Secretary General in ensuring international cooperation, the 8th MDG will remain what it is, a goal and targets, which will extend to the rest of the MDGs. On the other hand, full commitment to international cooperation by the G8 countries and the developing countries will provide a significant hope for the leaders of developing countries, for the more than 1.1 billion extremely poor and 1.6 billion[58] moderately poor members of the human race living in Sub Saharan Africa and worldwide.

Chapter Eleven

Conclusion

As an adult living in the global age, I look back from my childhood, on my journey through life thus far, satisfied that I asked the right questions. As for the answers I have got and given in these passages, I think they are just what we need as a people, a nation and a continent to join the world. I also think I need to write another book to answer other questions that arose when writing this piece.

I hope I have contributed well enough to focus our attention on the ills that came to the fore during the implementation of Washington Consensus policies in the 90s and to the solution to Africa's survival in the twenty-first century.

There are different perspectives on the prospects of Sub Saharan Africa in globalization. Scholars have not exhibited agreement and unity on the path that Africa should follow to first of all survive and then develop within the context of globalization. I hope my contribution to fill this gap in knowledge has been meaningful.

In fact, much literature by scholars concentrates upon the negative or positive consequences of globalization in Sub Saharan Africa. Some hold the view that globalization is just another form of the exploitation of Africa by the developed countries, that is former colonial masters; that it is just another form of imperialism.

Others hold the view that globalization is another way of perpetuating the position of Africa as an exporter of raw materials and a provider of market to and for the developed countries.

Still some authors argue that globalization provides Africa with the opportunity to develop. They hold that the increase in the flow of resources from the developed countries will ensure that economic and financial resources trickle down to Africa and other developing countries in the process. I agree with this only to the extent that Africa must not be a passive player waiting for the trickle down effect like manner from heaven.

In part, I agree with all the above views. I strongly believe that the diverse people that hold the diverse views above would agree with me that the first and most important step for Africa to survive in the twenty first century is for Sub Saharan Africans to have a cultural transformation of perspective, culture and behaviour with regard to presidentialism, ethnicity and clientelism and to high standard surplus productivity.

We need a cultural transformation that will help us run our societies responsibly with good attitudes, integrity and appreciation for the rule of law. Sub Saharan Africa requires a cultural transformation that will instil value for high standard surplus production of goods and services by taking an individual approach to development.

Globalization comes with both opportunities and challenges. It is up to individuals and African leaders to be pessimistic and complain about all the poor statistics to Sub Saharan Africa's credit or to be optimistic and do something about it.

Africa's eradication of poverty, achievement of economic growth and effective participation in international trade depends on a change in basic attitudes and engagement in surplus productivity in all areas, and that is what we should work on.

The evidence of the last ten to twenty years has demonstrated that attempting to implement the reforms of the *Washington Consensus* has ultimately proven to be a major economic success for the Asian Tigers and social disaster for developing countries of Sub Saharan Africa and Latin America.

The reason for their failure in Africa can among other factors be attributed more to low and low quality productivity and less to human error on the part of implementers as Williamson claims. According to Williamson [59]"The general ideas derived from the *Washington Consensus* had a huge influence on the economic reforms of many countries. Yet, the way these countries interpreted such ideas varied substantially and their actual implementation even more so."

To shed more light, I agree that the concepts were not understood until the end of the 90s. Few policy makers, technocrats and the general public understood the implications of the policies at the time until when the consequences were vividly evident. Implementation was too fast and the siphoning of public resources, done at individual level during the process was too large to merit any success of the policies.

A one individual at a time cultural transformation is therefore vital to ensure that a productive attitude and knowledge based society emerges and that corruption does not derail the implementation of my suggestions or any other policy.

Alongside this transformation should be the pursuit of the opportunities in international cooperation. These include the 0.7%, WTO agreements and debt eradication.

Once these basics are in place, Sub Saharan Africa to survive in the global village must develop an effective, extensive and comprehensive optic fibre telecommunication system. Globalization has come with it the information Age. Without access and control over a significant proportion of information, Sub Saharan Africa will not survive the global economy. Africa can come out of its cocoon in which it has dwelt for so long as a passive player in the global economy. It has remained behind in the use of information technology as a tool for business and development hence the lack of participation.

Globalization will always work to the benefit of those with ready access to information. Only those with information at their fingertips and that have control over it will prosper because globalization favours those who know what is affecting the markets and the global economy.

In this case, telecommunications infrastructure must be established that can electronically link all of Africa to itself and to other parts of the world. In other words, African electronic commerce (E- commerce) must be allowed to fully thrive and extensively develop. According to the former United Nations Conference on Trade and Development (UNCTAD) Secretary General, Rubens Ricupero,

> "E-commerce constitutes a major opportunity for trade and development. It can be a source of a significant number of success stories by which developing countries and their enterprises can reach new levels of international competitiveness and participate more actively in the global information economy."
>
> (Electronic Commerce Magazine).

Africa needs e-commerce not only to trade within itself but also with other countries. Effective communication and information systems can be vital for Africa to market its products and easily obtain more information and ideas about the strategies of other countries.

Electronic commerce transactions can certainly help Sub Saharan Africa overcome geographical isolation as a barrier to trade. By enhancing communications systems, Africa's proximity to global markets can provide an immediate global arena for African businessmen and women to negotiate and sell their goods to all parts of the world at reduced costs.

To further increase the flow of information, Africans must individually and collectively ensure they venture into research to unearth information on every aspect of the continent from economic to cultural to social to technological to the arts and to disseminate it quickly. Information must be made available especially to African citizens.

One can be convinced that if there are any barriers to totally break down in Africa, they are those that block access to information. If necessary, information must be forced upon all Africans. In the global village, ignorance is not bliss but a carcinogen of impoverishment. The old adage that knowledge is power proves true. Therefore, each African State can begin to embark on a policy of information, telecommunication and communication systems infrastructure development.

African leaders, businessmen and women, and influential people must also begin a widespread campaign to woo Africans to buy African-produced goods and services wherever they are. This is in order to secure Africa with a ready market for its goods and services. Under globalization, a country will survive and prosper if its private sector has adequate market for the goods produced. This campaign can also be extended to countries beyond the African border. With the prevailing sardonic view of Africa, the continent will face many hurdles in its efforts to secure markets. However, victory is certain on the condition that African products steadily increase in quality.

In addition to the above point, Sub Saharan African bureaucrats must be trained to administer African policies within the context of globalization. Bureaucracies usually set the pace for the development of any country and are usually slow. Globalization requires that bureaucrats work together with the private sector in the free market environment. Therefore, bureaucrats must be trained to work in a private sector driven economy including those in the rural sector economy. Above all, the private sector is a fast and versatile sector. In this regard, bureaucrats must be trained to adapt the characteristically slow bureaucracy to working in a fast, dynamic and versatile manner.

> I believe it is time for the lights to be lit in the Dark Continent that it may be called the bright continent and only we can do it. It is time to awaken the sleeping giant, it can be done.

Endnotes

[1] The Zambian Post Newspaper # 1934, Wednesday January 30, 2003

[2] World Bank. World Development Report 2002. New York: Oxford University Press

[3] WTO. World Trade Report 2005. Geneva

[4] Eban, Abba. 1998. _Diplomacy for the Next Century._ New Haven: Yale University Press. _Page 173_

[5] Eban, Abba. 1998. _Diplomacy for the Next Century._ New Haven: Yale University Press. _Page 174_

[6] UNAIDS & ECA. October 2000. _AIDS in Africa: Country by Country._ Geneva, Switzerland: UNAIDS

[7] Transparency International Report 2005

[8] Economic Commission for Africa. 2005. _Africa Governance Report 2005._ Addis Ababa. Page 22

[9] Van Der Veen, Roel. 2004. _What Went Wrong With Africa._ Amsterdam

[10] Riggs, Fred. "Conceptual Homogenisation of a Heterogeneous Field: Presidentialism in Comparative Perspective" in "Mattei, Dogan and Ali Kazancigil (eds) comparing Nations: Concepts, Strategies, Substance. Blackwell. 1994. pp72-152

[11] Mill, John Stuart. 1909. _Principles of Political Economy with some of their Application to Social Philosophy._ London: Green and Company

[12] Bulbula, Girma Yilma. _Ethnicism Hinders Africa's Development._ Executive Intelligence Review of June 20, 1997 _pp 65-66._ A presentation to a conference on "The Bretton Woods System and the Eurasian Land-Bridge", sponsored by the FDR-PAC in Seattle on June 5, 1997.

[13] Pareto, Vilfredo. 1963. _The Mind and Society: A Treaties on General Sociology._ New York. Harcourt Brace, New Edition. Page 1837

[14] Parsons, Talcott. 1975. "Some Theoretical Considerations on the Nature and Trends of Change of Ethnicity". In "Nathan Glazer and Daniel Moyniham (Eds) Ethnicity: Theory and Experience. Cambridge, Massachusetts. Harvard University Press. P 53

[15] Osaghae, E.E. 1992. "_Ethnicity, Class and the Struggle for State Power in Liberia_" A paper presented at the CODESRIA Conference on ethnic Conflict in Africa, Nairobi Kenya, November 1992

[16] William, Idowu. Ethnicity, Ethnicism and Citizenship: A theoretical Reflection on the African Experience 'in' Kamla Raj. 2004. _Journal of Social Sciences p45-58_

[17] Ibid

[18] Van Der Veen, Roel. 2004. _What Went Wrong With Africa._ Amsterdam: Kit Publishers _p102_

[19] Mwanakatwe, John. 1994. _End of Kaunda Era_. Lusaka: Multimedia Zambia _p86_

[20] Mwanakatwe, John. 1994. _End of Kaunda Era_. Lusaka: Multimedia Zambia _pp55-56_

[21] Van Der Veen, Roel. 2004. _What Went Wrong With Africa_. Amsterdam: Kit Publishers _p102_

[22] Bulbula, Girma Yilma. _Ethnicism Hinders Africa's Development_. Executive Intelligence Review of June 20, 1997 _pp 65-66_. A presentation to a conference on "The Bretton Woods System and the Eurasian Land-Bridge", sponsored by the FDR-PAC in Seattle on June 5, 1997.

[23] Naim, Moses (Ed) Fads and Fashion in Economic Reforms: Washington Consesnus or Washington Confusion? 'in' _Foreign Policy Magazine_ October 26, 1999, Washington D.C

[24] Naim, Moses (Ed) Fads and Fashion in Economic Reforms: Washington Consesnus or Washington Confusion? 'in' _Foreign Policy Magazine_ October 26, 1999, Washington D.C

[25] Gilpin, Robert. 2000. _The Challenge of Global Capitalism_. New Jersey: Princeton University Press

[26] Gilpin, Robert. 2000. _The Challenge of Global Capitalism_. New Jersey: Princeton University Press _pp232-233_

[27] Stiglitz, Joseph E. 2002. _Globalisation and Its Discontents_. London: Penguin Books Limited

[28] Rodney, Walter. 1982. _How Europe Underdeveloped Africa_. Macmillan Publishers

[29] The World Investment Directory 1996. Volume V. Africa. New York and Geneva: United Nations (1997)

[30] Todaro, Michael P. 1982. *Economics for a Developing World.* Princeton: Princeton University Press

[31] Stiglitz, Joseph E. 2002. *Globalisation and Its Discontents*. London: Penguin Press *p11*

[32] ibid

[33] Stiglitz, Joseph E. 2002. *Globalisation and Its Discontents*. London: Penguin Press *p9*

[34] Van Italie, Nancy L (Ed). 2000. *Model United Nations Conference Prepapration Handbook*. The Hague. *P73*

[35] World Trade Report 2004. Geneva: World Trade Organisation

[36] World Trade Report 2004. Geneva: World Trade Organisation

[37] African Recovery Magazine. May 2003: United Nations

[38] Ibid

[39] Op. Cit.

[40] UNDP. Human Development Report 2005. New York

[41] UNDP. Human Development Report 2005. New York

[42] UNDP. Human Development Report 2005. New York

[43] World Bank. World Development Report 2006. New York: United Nations

[44] UNDP. Human Development Report 2005. New York

[45] Mwanakatwe, John. 1994. *End of Kaunda Era*. Lusaka: Multimedia Publishers *p113*

[46] Mwanakatwe, John. 1994. *End of Kaunda Era*. Lusaka: Multimedia Publishers *p113*

[47] Sachs, Jefrey D. 2005. *The End of Poverty: How We Can Make it Happen in Our Lifetime.* London: Penguin Books

[48] The PANOS Briefing (No. 31. 1998)

[49] Africa Recovery Magazine. May 2003: United Nations *p4*

[50] World Investment Directory 1997. World Trade Organisation

[51] Government of the Republic of Zambia Country Country Presentation to the United Nations Least Developed Countries Conference 2001. *p19*

[52] Sachs, Jefrey D (ed) . 2005. *UN Millennium Project Report: Investing in Development; A Practical Plan to Achieve the Millennium Development Goals*. London: Earthscan

[53] Seldon, Anhony. 2005. *Blair*. London

[54] Patel, Dipak. 2005. *The Trinity of Aid, Fair Trade and Debt Relief.*
The Zambian Post Newspaper

[55] Sachs, Jefrey D. *Foreign Affairs,* March/April 2005 *p79*

[56] Sachs, Jeffrey D. 2005. *The End of Poverty: How we can Make it Happen in our Lifetime*. London: Penguin Books *p226*

[57] Annan, Kofi. In Larger Freedom: Decision Time 'in' *Foreign Affairs* April/June 2005

[58] Sachs, Jefrey D. 2005. *The End of Poverty: How We Can Make it in Our Lifetime*. London: Penguin Books *p20*

[59] Naim, Moses (Ed) Fads and Fashion in Economic Reforms: Washington Consensus or Washington Confusion? 'in' *Foreign Policy Magazine* October 26, 1999 Washington D.C

 Singumbe Muyeba was until recently an Expert on Mission for a GEF/UNDP funded Project in Zambia. He was also a United Nations Volunteer assigned to the same project. Prior to this, he worked in the Public Information Unit of the United Nations High Commissioner for Refugees (UNHCR). He holds a Bachelor of Arts Degree in the Social Sciences from the University of Zambia. He has published a number of articles in the print media, including one on Globalisation and the Eighth Millennium Development Goal, incorporated in this book as Chapter Ten. He is married to Abigail.